Real Spiritual Spinach

Faith for the Journey

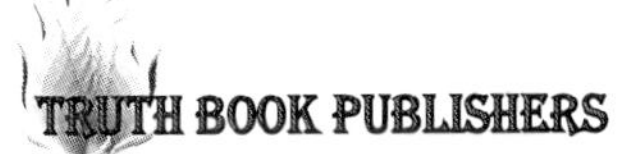

Tammy Real-McKeighan

Cover design by JaNell Lyle

ISBN: 978-1-935298-15-1 10: 1-935298-15-1

1. Books--Religion 2. Spritural 3. Self Help
1. Title

Truth Book Publishers
824 Bills Rd
Franklin, IL 62638
www.truthbookpublishers.com

Printed in the United States of America

The newspaper columns you love – now in book form.

Praise for "Real Spiritual Spinach – Faith for the Journey."

"Spiritual Spinach can help put some 'iron' into your faith! Tammy speaks from real life, with real faith, to real situations, for real people, out of real conviction – a genuine, loving, caring, authentic child of God writes to put some 'greens' in your spiritual diet! This is the real thing!" - **The Rev. Timothy Gierke, senior pastor, Good Shepherd Lutheran Church, Fremont.**

"Tammy writes with a warmth and genuineness that is refreshing in Spiritual Spinach. She insightfully looks at real life issues by combining wit, personal experience, and humor which truly touch the heart. She is as creative a person as I have seen with her pen!" - **The Rev. Mike Washburn, senior pastor, Full Life Assembly of God Church, Fremont.**

"It is a joy to read the stories of the Bible as Tammy Real-McKeighan applies them to our everyday life. I have used some of her quotes in my sermon messages." - **The Rev. Leland D. Foreman, senior pastor, First Baptist Church, Fremont.**

"Tammy has written a number of articles about people, events and things that are of concern to me personally. But the messages contained in her short essays touch me with warmth and encouragement like no other. She writes about her faith and how that faith functions as the prism through which she views the joys and trials of life. In reading her articles I have found peace, healing and a bolstering of my faith. And the way she uses everyday subjects to illustrate the invisible hand of God helps me become aware that God is always present and close."- **Father Owen Korte, senior pastor, St. Patrick's Catholic Church, Fremont.**

"Tammy McKeighan provides the entire community with spiritual guidance through her deep and insightful articles. Tammy navigates the often muddy waters of the spiritual life with well researched and edifying perspectives. It is refreshing to have a Christian with integrity, courageously address issues that will empower our daily lives." - **The Rev. Dr. William A. Lewis, senior pastor, The Presbyterian Church, Fremont.**

"Genuine! Tammy Real-McKeighan captures the simplicity of God's word as it comes to life in everyday situations ... just the way it is meant to be. Tammy's writing is a pure reflection of her life: honest, practical and FUN!" - **Scott Murrish, Ambassador of Vision, Royal Family Kids' Camps, Inc.**

Acknowledgments

I dedicate this book to my Lord and Savior Jesus Christ, whose very name gives me hope. I love you Lord.

And to my dear husband, Chuck, the love of my life and my "backboard" and my beloved children, Michael, and his wife, Rachel, and Zachary.

I am so thankful for my in-laws, Charles Sr. and Helen McKeighan, my dear aunts and uncles, nieces and nephews, and my family at Full Life Assembly of God Church in Fremont and, of course, my friends and fellow workers at the Fremont Tribune, who encourage me and make me laugh.

I owe much to the authors who have poured so much into my life and faith walk through their writings. They include Beth Moore, Max Lucado, Joyce Meyer, John C. Maxwell, Rick Warren and John Bevere.

I have a special thanks for my pals Martha Hartman, Nancy Ahrens, Doreen Beaudette, Debbie Rector, Sharon Steinbach and Toni Sorensen. And I'm very grateful to my buddy, Kandy Paulson, without whom this book might never have come about, and to Dr. William Keller, who always said that I should write a column.

In honor of Glenn and Evelyn Real and LuVerne Sawyer

Note to readers: How you may use this book

You certainly may read this book from front to back like other books. However, you also may use it like a devotional. Since each column is its own separate entity, you could read one a day for several days.

Or you could skip around to titles of columns that you think will interest you. If you do this, please take my advice and use a pencil or pen to mark a small "X" by the title of the column you've just read so you later won't start reading a column – then become frustrated because you've already read it.. Don't be surprised if God ministers to you through the column you think you'd be least interested in reading.

Before you read each column, pray that God uses it to speak to you. Pause after reading a Scripture. Let it soak into your soul. Read it aloud if you get a chance.

Remember: Nothing takes the place of God's word.

Real Spiritual Spinach

Faith for the Journey

To: Deb,
May God
bless you
mightily in the
days ahead!
Tammy
Real-McKeighan

Tammy Real-McKeighan

Table of Contents

What Makes Us Strong

I have a question for you.

What made Popeye strong?

Surely you remember the old Popeye cartoons. You can still see them once in awhile on TV.

Popeye, the sailor, carried a pipe in his mouth and bore the tattoo of an anchor on one of his meaty forearms. He had a spaghetti-thin girlfriend named Olive Oyl and a big, gruff nemesis called Bluto.

Somehow Bluto was always picking on Popeye, who'd end up tied up, chained up, beat up or otherwise down on his luck. Then Bluto would run off with Olive, who'd be screaming for help at the top of her lungs.

That's when Popeye would gulp down some spinach.

He was ingenious when it came to getting the stuff. He'd use his pipe as a blow torch to open the can or he'd slurp up the spinach through his pipe - or something.

Suddenly he'd become amazingly strong.

He'd punch Bluto and send him to the moon.

And Olive would be all over Popeye like fleas on a dog.

Just as spinach made Popeye strong, people today have an incredible source of strength.

May I suggest to you that the word of God - the Bible - is our spiritual spinach.

I know from experience that God speaks through his word. Even the Bible says "Man does not live by bread alone, but by every word that proceeds from the mouth of the father."

That's why I believe it's so important to read God's word.

And learn it.

Ohhh. I know. You hate memorization. I hate it, too. But we already memorize telephone numbers, passwords, song lyrics and the jingles to TV commercials.

Remember this: "Two all-beef patties, special sauce, lettuce, cheese, pickles, onions on a sesame seed bun"?*

It's ingredients to a Big Mac and I still remember the words I heard as a child.

In church, we sing some choruses that include music put to the words of a Bible verse. I've made up my own little tune for a Bible verse before as well. Nothing impressive, but functional.

In her DVD/workbook series, "Breaking Free - Making Liberty in Christ a Reality in Life," Christian speaker and author Beth Moore suggests writing Scriptures on index cards.*

I tried that. Know what? It works.

I wrote verses on cards and once every day said them out loud. That way I heard them with my ears and my heart. After about a week, I found I could say almost all of a verse without looking at the card. It didn't take much to fill in the words I would forget.

I believe it's also important to pray and ask God to help you remember the verses. The Bible talks about the Holy Spirit reminding us of God's word. I've found that to be true on many occasions.

Can I tell you how wonderful it is to be going through a tough time and have those verses come to mind?

There's one verse that I especially find dear, because I've lived it so thoroughly.

Years ago, I was a single mother coming home from a friend's house in Scribner. Life was hard. I was filled with weariness and anxiety. It was night when I reached the outskirts of Fremont and saw the city's line of colored lights on the horizon. I remember praying, "Please God, you've got to help me. You've got to let me know that my life isn't going to end in calamity. You've got to give me some kind of hope for the future."

The next night I went to a women's retreat at my church where the speaker talked about the "desert times" of life - those times when we don't know if we're going to make it or not.

Then she recited a verse. It was Jeremiah 29:11: "For I know the plans I have for you says the Lord of hosts, plans to help and not harm you. Plans to give you hope and a future."

It sounded nice, but the full impact didn't hit me until the next day when a friend asked me how the retreat went.

"Oh, they talked about this cool verse....," I said before starting to read it to her.

I barely made it through. The words jumped right off the page and into my heart as I realized God had answered my prayer almost word for word - with a promise. He had plans of hope and a future for me.

I hung up the phone and wept. It was as if God was saying, "You're going to be OK, Tammy."

So whenever I felt very alone and afraid, I repeated that verse to myself.

Today, I am walking, breathing, living proof of God's faithfulness and that bad times can get better. I have a wonderful husband, two great sons, a fine daughter-in-law and more blessings than I'm sure I will ever realize.

And I know that whenever discouragement, fear or sadness come at me like a big, crabby, old Bluto, I just give it the one-two punch by saying one of the verses that have become so priceless to me.

I think Popeye would be proud.

*From McDonald's restaurants commercial

*Used by permission of Lifeway Christian Resources.

Facing Lions

I remember the scene well.

I walked into the bedroom after hearing that my husband might be losing his job - right before Christmas.

It wasn't his fault. New management was taking over. And my husband figured they'd lay off pretty much everyone.

Fear rose up inside of me like water on a sinking ship.

That's when I prayed, "God, you've got to talk to me."

I sat on the bed and opened the Bible. Paging through I began looking for some verses that would bring comfort, peace or hope.

Then I came across the story of Daniel and the lions den.

Now, I know the story pretty well.

Daniel was a young Hebrew, taken into captivity by the Babylonians. Throughout the years, he consistently impressed top leaders who promoted him to positions of authority.

There was just one problem. He reached a point where his Babylonian counterparts became jealous. So they conspired to get rid of him and tricked the king into sending Daniel to what surely would be his death in a den of lions.

Daniel was tossed into the den which was shut with a rock.

There he was.

With the lions.

Alone.

In my imagination I could almost picture myself with Daniel, looking at those lions.

See that lion over there?

His name is Fear and he's going to chew me up.

See that other one over there?

His name is Doubt and he's going to rip me to shreds with his claws.

See still another one?

His name is Despair and he'll finish off what the other two started.

But then I had to read the rest of the story.

What happened next?

The king worried all night about Daniel. He liked the guy. He didn't want this to happen.

So the next morning he hurried to the den and had it opened.

There was Daniel.

Still in one piece.

How did this happen?

"My God sent his angel and he shut the mouths of the lions," Daniel told the king, who was overjoyed and had the prophet pulled from the pit.

I love what I read next about Daniel.

"No wound was found on him, because he had trusted in his God."

I guess Daniel wasn't alone.

A thought hit me as I imagined myself standing before those lions of fear and doubt in that dark den.

Who shut the lions' mouths?

Yep. It was God.

Then I prayed, "Lord, please shut the lions' mouths!"

And the most amazing thing happened.

A feeling of peace flooded my soul - and remained.

My husband didn't lose his job before Christmas.

He lost it afterward.

But he found another, then studied very hard and passed a test that paved the way for the job he has now. It's a good job.

So what did I learn through all this?

I learned that while we may not live in ancient times, we still face lions of some sort. They can be big and threatening and scary.

But that's when I have to remember who keeps them in place.

And who brings peace to our souls.

Blow Your Nose, Then Sing

If you're like me and suffer from seasonal allergies, then you can relate to these symptoms:

Your nose is as red as a Roma tomato and it burns every time you blow it. You cough until your throat is sore. You wonder who sneaked around and filled your sinuses with lead.

And you figure there must be slugs with more energy than you.

I was like that the other day. That's when I needed a good first aid type Scripture from a prophet named Isaiah.

The verse that began filtering through my thick brain was this:

"They who wait upon the Lord shall renew their strength; they shall mount up with wings as eagles; they shall run and not be weary; they shall walk and not faint." It is found in the Old Testament book of Isaiah, chapter 40, verse 31.

Now, Isaiah was no doctor, but I've seen that verse infuse people with healing, encouragement and energy.

Are you weary from overwork ... taking care of a sick loved one ... trying to raise your grandchildren?

Then write this verse on a piece of paper and put it on your refrigerator or near the bathroom mirror. Say it out loud to yourself. It's a promise from God.

Besides this verse, a Bible story came to mind during my allergy battle.

It's the New Testament one where Paul, the apostle, and his sidekick Silas are severely beaten and thrown in prison. The two are put in a cell and their feet are fastened with stocks.

Talk about feeling terrible. You think they'd be angry, complaining or, at least, whimpering a little.

Not these guys.

Around midnight, they're praying and singing hymns to God. And other prisoners are listening.

Then God does the marvelous.

He sends an earthquake that shakes the prison's foundations. Prison doors fly open and everyone's chains come loose. The jailer just knows he's going to be held responsible for the biggest prison break in town - and prepares to kill himself.

But Paul stops him.

"Don't harm yourself. We're all here," he says.

At that point, the jailer falls to his knees and asks how he can be saved.

"Believe in the Lord Jesus, and you will be saved - you and your household," Paul says.

He and Silas do other teaching and the jailer even washes their wounds.

It's an astounding story. But one of the things I find most amazing is how God shook the prison's foundations.

When was the last time God rocked your world - and turned around a situation you thought was hopeless?

He can do that you know. Not just for Paul and Silas, but for people locked in a prison of unforgiveness, fear or grief. I've seen it and experienced it. You just have to ask him to help you and trust that he will.

Speaking of trust, I started singing a little during my miserable time with allergies. My singing was flat and probably resembled a comedy routine, but it made me feel better.

Then I remembered some medicine the doctor prescribed the last time I had a nasty bout with allergies that the over-the-counter stuff couldn't help. I called him. He called the pharmacy and God blessed me with a prescription that cost a whopping $4.82.

I've started feeling better. But what makes me feel the best is the knowledge that God loves me and is with me - through runny noses and sagging sinuses.

And really bad singing.

Lessons from a Rock Thrower

I have always loved the story of David and Goliath.

Enfolded in the story of a young shepherd who defeats a giant are a multitude of lessons that continue to inspire me.

The story begins after David comes to the site of an impending battle between the Israelites and the Philistines. The scene starts at two hills. King Saul and the Israelites are on one hill and the Philistines on the other.

Only a valley separates them.

David's three oldest brothers have been sent to the battle. There, they and other Israelites see Goliath of Gath, a 9-foot-tall warrior with a bad temper and a big mouth. Goliath shouts at Israel's ranks. He wants them to choose a man to fight him. If the Israelites win, then the Philistines will be their servants.

But if Goliath wins, then the Israelites will become the Philistines' slaves.

Goliath takes his stand every day for 40 days.

The Israelites are terrified.

Now comes the time for some great lessons.

Here are some things I've learned:

*** Don't let others discourage you.** David's brother became angry when the young boy came to the scene and started asking what all the shouting was about. He called David "conceited." Later, even the king tried to dissuade David from fighting Goliath by telling him the odds.

"You're only a boy and he's been a fighting man from his youth," Saul said.

Such talk didn't stop David.

I love how pastors and other speakers define this moment: "Most people saw Goliath as a foe too big to defeat. David saw him as a target too big to miss."

*** Trust God**. God had prepared David to meet Goliath. Long before David ever put his sandaled feet on that battlefield, he'd experienced God's faithfulness as a shepherd boy.

"When a lion or a bear came and carried off a sheep from the flock, I went after it, struck it and rescued the sheep from its mouth. When it turned on me, I seized it by its hair, struck it and killed it," he said.

OK. Wait a minute. This is a lion and bear we're talking about. I shudder to think about the large lions I've seen in zoos. Or the big bears I've seen in movies.

I don't think I'd want to be pulling their hair.

But David had found his confidence in God. He knew God wouldn't let him down.

"The God who delivered me from the paw of the lion and the paw of the bear will deliver me from the hand of this Philistine," he said.

*** Use the method that works for you.** When King Saul agreed to let David meet the giant, he put his own armor on the boy. David tried walking around in it, but took it off because he wasn't used to it. Then he chose five smooth stones from a stream, put them in his shepherd's bag and with a sling in his hand went to meet Goliath.

*** Remember who's really running the show.** When Goliath saw David, he despised the boy and started hurling insults like javelins. But somehow they bounced off David, who wasn't going to let this big, crabby guy insult God or his army anymore.

"This day, the Lord will hand you over to me .... All those gathered here will know that it is not by the sword or spear that the Lord saves: for the battle is the Lord's ...."

What incredibly powerful fighting words.

Then David ran - not walked - to meet his opponent.

Many Sunday school children can tell you the rest of the story - how David hurled a stone at Goliath and stuck him in the forehead. Goliath fell face down and died. The Philistines ran off and David was a hero.

Actually, God is the real hero of the story.

And here's perhaps the best lesson of all:

We may never face a 9-foot-tall giant, but there are times in our lives when our problems seem every bit as big and hairy and threatening as that giant.

That's when we have to remember that little shepherd kid and who was on his side.

A Recipe for Forgiveness

I have a confession.

I've had my share of cooking fiascoes.

Now, not everything I've made has turned out badly, but what did sure left an impression.

There was the time my husband, Chuck, and I were given "Brownies in a Jar" as a gift.

It was so pretty. Layers of sugar, chocolate chips and other dry ingredients looked like a sandpainting inside the glass jar. A checkered cloth top with the recipe just added to the homey effect.

One day I decided to make those brownies, unaware of a typo in the recipe.

I thought it was strange when I read: "1/2 cap of oil," but figured these jar brownies must be different than the store-bought kind.

So using the cap on the vegetable oil bottle, I carefully measured out my 1/2 cap of oil. I whipped up the batch and put it in the oven.

I told Chuck about the brownies when he called me on the way home. You should have heard the desperation in his voice.

"No Tammy. Not one-half cap. It should be one-half cup...."

Oops.

I pulled the brownies out of the oven. It still amazes me how brownies with so little oil still ended up looking like sludge. You'd have thought the Exxon Valdez crashed into my baking pan. No amount of baking saved them and not even our hungry nephew could stomach them.

I think it's safe to say that I'm probably not the person to go to for cooking tips. But if you want a recipe for forgiveness, I might be able to help you.

Here are some tips that have helped me:

*** Tell God how the person hurt you and ask the Lord to heal the hurt in your heart.** Ask him to help you forgive this person. Don't try to do it in your own strength. We need the Holy Spirit to help us. Make a decision to forgive and ask God to help you stick to that decision.

Now try to remember that:

*** Most people aren't trying to hurt someone.** Many may not even know they've hit a nerve with you. Sometimes people say things because they're trying to be funny or sound ultra intelligent. They may not realize until later what they've said, then may be afraid to say something else for fear of making it worse.

*** "Hurting people hurt people."** I don't know where Christian author Joyce Meyer got this phrase, but she's repeated it in her broadcasts. Many times people lash out because of their own pain.

*** Forgiving someone doesn't make what they did right**. It just frees you. Christian author Beth Moore discusses this in her DVD/workbook series, "Living Beyond Yourself - Exploring the Fruit of the Spirit."*

And as someone who was molested as a child, she should know.

*** Bitterness and unforgiveness only hurts you**. Meyer, who also was molested as a child, generally says something like this: "Harboring unforgiveness is like drinking poison and hoping that it kills your enemy."

*** It's not up to us to take revenge**. Romans 12:19 says "Do not take revenge, my friends, but leave room for God's wrath, for it is written: 'It is mine to avenge; I will repay,' says the Lord."

*** God has forgiven us so we need to do the same.** Remember Jesus' parable of the unmerciful servant? Matthew 18: 23-35 tells of a king who forgave a tremendous debt to a servant. But that man, in turn, threw a fellow servant in prison for a much smaller debt.

The king was furious when he learned about the first servant's lack of mercy and had him handed "over to the jailers to be tortured, until he should pay back all he owed."

It's easy to tell that the king in the story represents God, who has forgiven us so much, and how we can be that unmerciful servant - holding a grudge against someone who has wronged us far less?

Oh and what torture it is when we hold onto that unforgiveness.

I've personally lost sleep as I've wrestled with it in the past. I've seen others suffer physical ailments because of it.

And I know that unforgiveness can harden a heart more than anything I could overcook in the oven or burn on the grill.

It's been said that revenge is a dish best served cold. If that's true, then forgiveness is a dish best served warm with the love of Christ who died so we all could be forgiven.

*Used by permission of Lifeway Christian Resources

A Dog Named Ring

When I was growing up, my dad talked about two dogs.

One was Skippy, a dog he and Mom had on the farm when I was little.

The other was Ring.

Ring. I love the name. It reminds me of God and of a circle - no beginning, no ending, everlasting and complete.

No one tells story of Ring better than my aunt, Ena R. Carlson Wason. In her book, "Onions in the Stew," she shares what life was like for children of the Great Depression.

My dad, whose name was Glenn, my aunts Ena and Betty and uncle Frank lived on a farm in Nebraska during those difficult years. They were well acquainted with pastures that were home to squirrels and rabbits, coyotes and rattlesnakes. And they knew what it was to love a dog who was their friend and protector.

*****

It happened in August, Ena writes. I remember because it was close to my birthday. Glenn, Frank, Betty and I were on the way to the cow pasture to sort out and round up milk cows from the rest of the herd and bring the milkers into the corral ...

We were all barefoot.

It was late afternoon. The sun had not yet dipped behind the horizon, had not yet lowered the wattage on its dazzling rays and the heat was creating mirages, distortions, wavering lines, making it possible to see a snake that was not there and to miss one that was.

Frank was carrying the long-handled hoe, our anti-rattler artillery, which Mom unfailingly directed us to do....

Ring, our dog, part border collie, part blue heeler and certainly parts of other breeds, was trotting alongside Frank. Ring had a long, silky black coat. He had white paws and a snowy white circle around his neck ... We named him Ring.

Ring loved going to the pasture after the milkers. Dad liked having him go because on command Ring could cut a cow from the herd without nipping her heels. Our dog could bring in even the most reluctant bossie, reluctant because in August buffalo grass was pretty dry and should a cow find a succulent patch she could be stubbornly unwilling to leave it for any of her peers to chomp.

Mom liked having Ring go with us because our dog was a snake-killer and the pastures were crawling with snakes....

Ring was panting, his long wet tongue hanging out. He'd been chasing a rabbit and had just come back on duty.

Like brushes hitting a snare drum, the snake issued its warning. Ring saw the deadly reptile before we kids did. Our dog stiffened, crouched, and the hair rose on the back of his neck. A low rumble began in his throat.

Grrrrr....

"Snake!" Frank yelled, and raised the hoe into battle position, over his shoulder.

The snake was a big one. Lying coiled on a large limestone rock, his rattle was straight up, vibrating rapidly. After all the years between then and now, in my mind's eye I see the thick gray coil, the snake's triangular head, his slanted, hooded eyes and the pits in the back of them, his forked tongue, darting in and out of his mouth, his fangs.

He was less than a yard away from Glenn, who stood frozen and staring.

The snake struck out and Glenn drew back in horror, threw his hands up in front of his face and screamed a long, loud, blood-curdling scream.

Ring sprang between the boy and the snake. The rattler sank its fangs deep into the soft tissue just below Ring's nose and clung there. Ring shuddered and began shaking his head vigorously, back and forth, up and down, in an effort to rid himself of his attacker.

Frank's eyes filled, ran over, the tears streamed down his dusty, sunburned cheeks as he hacked with all of his strength at the writhing, gristly snake, doing all he could to miss hitting our dog. Finally, the snake released its hold and Glenn bent over and picked Ring up.

Our dog was limp and whimpering. Slowly, Glenn started for the house....

Frank continued chopping until he was absolutely certain this rattler would never strike anything again and then he took off, full speed, toward home.

Betty and I were bawling. "Oh, Ring. Ring. Ring."

Glenn, his small boy body wracked with sobs, his legs bent from the weight of the nearly unconscious, moaning animal, carried our dog in his arms. He cradled him like an infant, speaking to him, "Ring. Ring. Don't die. Please, don't die."

Frank raced ahead, yelling, waving the hoe high in the air.

Dad was in the yard, refueling the John Deere.

"Dad! Dad! snake...."

Dad took Ring from Glenn's arms and gently laid our dog in the tack shed, in the coolest corner. Ring's face was enormously swollen, his whimpering heartrending.

I had never seen my father weep before.

"Give him whiskey," our neighbor, Herman Larsen, said.

Dad made a special trip to town to buy a half pint of whiskey, but Ring's mouth was swollen shut. Ring lived three more days, moaning in agony while we kids paced and prayed and cried outside the tack shed.

Then, he died.

Dad buried Ring beneath the cottonwood tree, in the shade. He emptied the whiskey into the horse tank and tossed the bottle in the trash barrel to be burned....

We had other dogs, several of them. We never had another Ring."

*****

I have read this story many times and it still makes me cry. But years ago, I noticed something else. Just like Ring jumped in between that snake and my Dad, Jesus stood in between that cruel old snake we call the devil - and took the bite that was meant for us.

Unlike Ring, who died after three days, Jesus rose on the third day to bring us eternal life and hope.

Ring has been gone for decades. My dad died 12 years ago.

Now, I don't know if dogs go to heaven, but in my imagination I like to picture my Dad sitting on a grassy slope with his arm around a black dog with a white ring around its neck.

Better yet, I picture my Dad with his arm around the savior of his soul - our beloved Lord Jesus.

Walking on Water

Have you ever taught Sunday school?

Children's church or vacation Bible school?

If you haven't, may I suggest that you try it sometime?

Not only can you help children learn about God, but you might pick up a few lessons that can help you greatly in life.

I can't tell you how many Bible stories I learned - and were reminded of - while teaching little kids.

And those lessons continue to comfort, soothe and guide me.

One example happened last summer while Kathy Howerton, the children's director at my church, was teaching vacation Bible school.

During one session, she was telling the story of Jesus walking on the water.

You probably know the story. It can be found in chapter 14 of the New Testament book of Matthew.

In this account, Jesus sends his disciples off in a boat while he goes by himself to a mountainside to pray. After a while the boat is buffeted by the waves and the wind is against it.

Jesus begins walking on the water toward the boat. When the disciples see him, they become terrified because they think they're seeing a ghost.

But he immediately reassures them saying, "Take courage. It is I. Don't be afraid."

Peter - one of Jesus' followers - suddenly says "Lord, if it's you, tell me to come to you on the water."

Jesus tells him to come.

So Peter gets out of the boat and walks on water toward Christ.

But then Peter sees the wind, becomes afraid and starts to sink.

"Lord, save me," he cries out.

Immediately, Jesus reaches out his hand and catches Peter.

"You of little faith," Jesus says. "Why did you doubt?"

After Kathy told the story, she asked the children a question I've heard more than once. She wanted to know when Peter started to sink.

It was after he took his eyes off Jesus and started looking at the wind around him.

The lesson we can learn is that when we start focusing on the storms in our lives instead of Christ, we can begin to sink into the deep waters of fear, despair and frustration.

I was reminded of that lesson when I recently faced an unsettling situation. I had just learned some unnerving news.

I tried to stay calm so I wouldn't alarm those around me.

But my insides were starting to quake a little bit.

Then I suddenly got a mental picture of Kathy, standing in front of those children, reminding them to keep their eyes on Jesus.

It was a good reminder for me, too.

As adults we know there will always be the cold winds of job loss, financial crisis, sickness and death of loved ones.

That's when we need to remember the Lord who's always with us and who says "Take courage .... Don't be afraid."

That same Lord lets us step out of the boat - where it's safe - and do something we've never done before.

Something that can be life-changing and amazing.

And it's the same Lord who reaches out his hand and catches us when we cry out to him for help.

Did you notice that Peter didn't wait until he was almost under water to cry out to Christ? He was just beginning to sink when he sought Jesus.

Maybe that's a good reminder for us, as well. I wonder how much fear could be lessened and problems avoided if we prayed at the first hint of trouble.

At any rate, I hope the children in Kathy's class will remember this lesson, especially when they face tough times in life.

And I hope that as adults we always remember how God honors child-like faith.

It's certainly a lesson we can pass on to future generations.

God and Chelsea's Ham

Will there be enough?

It's a common question.

Will we have enough money to make it to payday?

Will there be enough gas in the car to last until the end of the week?

Will we have enough money for retirement?

How many times do we look at our finances, our supplies - even our strength - and wonder if we will have enough?

Chelsea Henrickson looked at the small box of donated ham and wondered if the church would have enough to feed 300 people at a funeral dinner. A young man had died unexpectedly in the North Dakota town where Chelsea and her family lived.

Altogether, five women worked through the night to prepare a meal for the next day. Since the church had limited resources, one worker called a frozen food company which donated a box of ham. It wasn't a whole ham. It was more like thick slices or chunks.

Chelsea figures they had about 8 pounds of ham.

The women bought rolls to make ham sandwiches. They prepared au gratin potatoes, cole slaw, green beans and pumpkin bars. They worked until about 1 or 2 a.m.

They returned at 9 a.m., heated and served the food.

"We fed everyone and called out for seconds. Many people passed through the line again. When all was said and done, we'd fed just over 300 people and had enough leftovers to provide complete meals for each of the five ladies' families," Chelsea said.

Sounds like a lot of people were fed from that ham. But since no one usually asks me to do the math, I called Jerry Abrahamson, owner of Jerry's Hometown Meats in Fremont.

Normally, he said, you get about five sandwiches to a pound of meat.

OK, multiply eight times five and you get 40 sandwiches.

Let's stretch the recipe.

If you only use 2 ounces of meat, you probably could get eight sandwiches to a pound of meat, he said.

Eight times eight is 64 sandwiches.

"There's no way you could feed 300," he said.

So how was there enough ham to feed all those people?

"I think it was miraculously multiplied," said Chelsea, now of Fremont.

I would agree.

What's more, Chelsea's story reminds me of one in the Bible in which Jesus miraculously feeds 5,000 people from five loaves of bread and two fish. The story, found in Matthew chapter 14, even tells about leftovers.

"They all ate and were satisfied, and the disciples picked up 12 basketfuls of broken pieces that were left over," the text says.

Think about that. Twelve baskets. Jesus had 12 close disciples. Do you think he was trying to teach each of them a personal lesson about trusting God? I wonder. But one thing I do know: The Bible has several stories of God's provision.

One of my favorites is found in 1 Kings, chapter 17. There is drought and famine in the land when God tells the prophet Elijah to go to the town of Zarephath. There, God has commanded a widow to feed Elijah.

Elijah finds her and asks for a piece of bread.

But she doesn't have any. She just has a handful of flour in a jar and a little oil in a jug. She plans to make one last meal for herself and her son, then she figures they'll starve to death.

Elijah tells her not to be afraid and to make bread for him - then for herself and her son. He says God has told him that the flour and oil won't be used up until he sends rain.

So she cooks for Elijah. Guess what happens? The oil and flour lasts until it rains.

How long was that? Well, the Bible says it didn't rain for 3 1/2 years. I'm not sure when during that period Elijah met the widow, but I'm guessing he stayed with her for quite a while.

Sounds like a lot of meals came from a handful of flour and little oil.

Today as I think about these Bible stories, I'm so glad I can hear about modern-day versions like Chelsea's.

And I think that whenever we're in a jam, we need to turn to the God who really knows how to stretch out a meal.

Never Give Up

I admire persistent people.

And one of the most tenacious I've ever heard of comes from the book, "Old Peninsula Days," by H.R. Holand. (North Word Press, Inc. 1959.)

The book, which tells the history of the Wisconsin region, shares the story of a young man who got lost in a blinding snowstorm on New Year's Day in 1864. He went days without food, sleep or heat.

At one point, he fell into a lake and was pulled under the ice. After a heroic struggle, he resurfaced but couldn't get back onto the fragile ice.

So, "he stayed in the freezing water, using his ice-encased arms and hands as sledgehammers to smash the thin ice and open a passage."

He slowly moved forward, half swimming, half crawling, for hours. Time after time, he thought he was lost, "but again and again, he conquered, smashing, plunging, rolling and swimming with temperatures at 40 degrees below zero."

His rescuers made the mistake of putting his limbs in kerosene. He was in pain for months and lost his arms. But later, with the help of artificial limbs, he continued a well-drilling business, never seeking favors because of his disability.

This story reminds me of another in the Bible about a blind man named Bartimaeus. The account is found in the 10th chapter of the New Testament book of Mark, starting with verse 46.

In the story, Jesus, his disciples and a large crowd were leaving Jericho.

Bartimaeus was sitting by the roadside, begging. When he heard that Jesus was coming, Bartimaeus began to shout, "Jesus, son of David, have mercy on me!"

Now, you'd think the crowd would have had compassion for a

blind man crying out to Christ. But they told him to be quiet.

That didn't stop him, though. He shouted all the more.

Jesus stopped and told the group to call Bartimaeus over to him. Suddenly, the crowd changed its tune. "Cheer up. On your feet. He's calling for you," they said.

Bartimaeus wasted no time. He threw his cloak aside, jumped to his feet and came to Jesus.

Then Jesus asked what might seem a strange question:

"What do you want me to do for you?"

You'd think it would be obvious. But maybe Jesus needed the man to clarify the desire in his own heart. Or maybe Christ wanted others standing nearby to hear the depth of this man's need. Either way, I can hear tenderness mixed with authority in Jesus' words: "Go, your faith has healed you."

Bartimaeus immediately received his sight and started following Jesus along the road.

As I read this story, I wonder what would have happened if Bartimaeus had given up when others told him to be quiet. Would he have ever known the joy of sight? Or would he have died full of regret for not having tried a little harder?

I personally believe that Bartimaeus was so tired of being in such a miserable situation that he was desperate enough to do what it took to get help. And he got it when he cried out to the only one who could really help him.

Perseverance is never an easy thing, but it brings rewards.

I know because I've experienced it.

Many years go, I was struggling in my job. It seemed like everything that could go wrong did go wrong. My many inadequacies were painfully obvious. Deep down inside I was so fearful that I couldn't even let myself think about the worst - being let go.

At times, I wondered if I should just find another job, but I couldn't imagine how I could get a good recommendation to get one.

I knew I'd have to get things straightened out. So by the amazing grace God, I hung in there. It was tough for a very long, hard time. Day after day, I asked God to make the next day better. Day after day, it seemed like nothing changed.

I felt like I was walking through a fog.

Then the fog began to lift. Circumstances slowly started to change. I learned and grew in my job.

I am so blessed. Today, I really believe I have one of the best jobs around. What if I'd quit? I really wonder if God would have let me.

And maybe that's the way it was for Bartimaeus.

Maybe it was the spirit of God nudging him on, telling him to "go for it" and not to give up.

One of the things I love about Bartimaeus is that he didn't get rude with the naysayers around him. He didn't try to tell them off. He just kept his focus on his source of help.

And I believe, that in the end, Bartimaeus gained so much more than physical sight.

He got a glimpse - heavenly insight - of the awesome power of God.

A Little Spilled Milk

Ever heard the phrase, "waiting on God"?

It means to wait for God to work out his plan for your life - instead of trying to help him do his job.

It's tough and it's one of the hardest lessons I've ever had to learn.

My "studies on waiting" hit an interesting chapter around the year 1980 B.C. - that's Before Chuck (my husband) - when I was a student at Midland Lutheran College. Back then, I worked in the cafeteria. Part of my job was to double check student numbers as kids came through the lunch line.

One day, a guy caught my attention. He had curly hair and big blue eyes and looked like one of those perfect statues from my art history books. At the time I was single and looking for Mr. Right.

I thought I might have found him. So I'd purposely mess up his number just to get a better look at him.

He probably thought I was an idiot.

After I'd eaten my dinner one evening, I decided to get his attention.

My roommate, Deb, and I were sitting at a table not far from this guy and his friends. I figured I'd walk past his table on my way to get a glass of milk - hoping to catch his eye on the return trip.

I planned to give him a big smile.

With Deb watching, I meandered past the guy's table, got my milk and walked back.

He was shoveling beef stew into his mouth and never even looked up.

Undaunted, I decided to get another glass. But this time, on the way back to the table, my foot slipped. I didn't fall, but I dumped the milk all down the front of myself.

I got a nice round of applause from a group of guy basketball players sitting at another table.

Obviously, they were impressed by my athletic display.

But the curly-haired guy never looked up.

One of the basketball players helped me wipe up the mess. Then, suddenly, I realized I was late for my philosophy class - and we were taking a test.

Guess who smelled like sour milk during her test?

What happened to the curly-haired guy? I found out he was trying to date a pretty girl in our dormitory.

Hmmm.

I wonder what would have happened if I'd done a better job of waiting for God to bring Mr. Right into my life.

As time progressed, my inability to wait on the Lord produced more than one painful lesson. And looking back, I don't know why I thought the God of the universe couldn't handle the situation.

Don't get me wrong. I know waiting is difficult - especially when it involves years.

But I also know God has our best interests at heart.

So as I grew in my faith I learned to cling to verses like: "Take delight in the Lord and he will give you the desires of your heart." Psalm 37:4.

I also read about a single guy we know as the Apostle Paul who wrote: "I have learned the secret of being content in any and every situation, whether well fed or hungry, whether living in plenty or in want."

Notice the word "learned." Paul says he learned how to be content. It obviously didn't happen overnight.

So how did I begin to fill the empty, aching void in my heart?

Well, God did, actually, as I put him first in my life by praying to him and reading his word.

I told him repeatedly about the longings in my heart and started trusting him.

I got involved in lots of church activities, made great, supportive friends and saw my faith grow.

Looking back, I'm grateful that the curly-haired guy never

looked up from his stew. He might have been horrified at the sight of a milk-soaked girl.

And I might have gotten involved with the wrong guy.

Instead, I'm thankful that God is so much smarter than I am. He found me the perfect mate: My husband, Chuck.

Am I crying over a little spilled milk these days?

Not a chance.

Willie and Joe and King Jehoshaphat

When I was a child, my dad was a truck driver.

Now, lots of truck drivers have stories and jokes to tell.

My dad never told many jokes, but one that I remember was about two imaginary truckers named Joe and Willie.

The joke went something like this:

Joe and Willie were being interviewed by a reporter one day.

The reporter asked Joe, "What if were you were driving and Willie was sleeping and you were going down a hill and the brakes went out? And worse yet, there were ditches and a line of trees on each side of the road - and at the end of the road was a train on the tracks?"

Joe thought for a minute.

"I think I'd wake Willie," he said.

"Why would you wake Willie?" the reporter asked.

"'Cuz Willie ain't never seen an accident like this one we're fixin' to have."

I still smile at my Dad's old joke, but it also makes me think how often we worry about things that may never happen.

I've done a lot of that in my life and recently fell into that bad habit again. It happened after I kind of got myself into a little mess and wondered what I would do next. I imagined all sorts of scenarios - from mildly uncomfortable to almost awful.

I was praying about the situation in church one Sunday when my pastor's wife, Terry Washburn, started telling why we should worship God.

Her comments reminded me of my all-time favorite Old Testament story. It's found in 2 Chronicles, chapter 20, of the Bible.

In this account, King Jehoshaphat was facing terrible situation. Three enemy groups had formed a big army and planned to attack the King of Judah and his people.

The people gathered and Jehoshaphat prayed. He acknowledged God's power during his prayer. At the end, he prayed: "For we have no power to face this vast army that is attacking us. We do not know what to do, but our eyes are on you."

What a great example!

When we don't know what to do - or even when we think we do - we should keep our focus on God.

After the king's prayer, the spirit of the Lord came upon one man, who in part, proclaimed: "This is what the Lord says to you: "Do not be afraid or discouraged because of this vast army. For the battle is not yours but God's."

The man then told the people where they should go to meet this army, but again said they wouldn't have to fight.

"Take up your positions; stand firm and see the deliverance the Lord will give you."

King Jehoshaphat bowed with his face to the ground after he heard the news. Early the next morning, he encouraged his people by saying, "Have faith in the Lord your God and you will be upheld."

Then he appointed men to go out ahead of the army and sing.

Sing?

Yep.

Can you imagine former Gen. Norman Schwarzkopf sending a men's choir to go ahead of the U.S. Army at the start of Desert Storm?

Neither can I.

But as Jehoshaphat's appointees began to sing and praise, God set ambushes against the enemies - who ended up destroying each other.

By the time the men of Judah reached a place that overlooked the desert, they saw only the dead bodies of the vast army on the ground.

No one had escaped.

It took Jehoshaphat and his men three days to carry away the plunder.

Imagine that.

They got some good praise music and some lovely parting gifts.

Afterward, the Bible says that the fear of God came upon the kingdoms of the other countries when they heard how the Lord fought against the enemies of Israel.

"And the kingdom of Jehoshaphat was at peace for his God had given him rest on every side."

Once I recalled that story, I started to thank and praise God - not as some sort of formula or bribe - but just because I know that in my own life, he's defeated armies whose soldiers were fear, stress and doubt.

A couple of days passed. But instead of trying to jump in and "fix" everything - most likely just making it worse - I prayed, trusted in God and waited.

And then God did it.

He worked out my problem in a wonderful way. With a grateful heart, I told him thank you.

Now I guess there's just one thing left to do.

I think I'll wake Willie.

Why?

'Cuz Willie ain't never seen a miracle like this one I just had.'

Welcome to Goshen

Note: I wrote this column when gas prices were $4 a gallon, but I still believe it holds true today.

I have a news flash for you:

There is hope.

I know. You've read all the reports of rising gas prices, tremendous consumer debt and a recession looming on the horizon. Maybe you're struggling financially. Maybe big time.

It's enough to make even the most stalwart Christian a little queasy.

But nothing is hopeless - not with God in the picture.

Lately, I've been reading about Joseph in the Bible. Not as in Jesus' parents, Joseph and Mary, in the New Testament. This Joseph is in the Old Testament. This is the Joseph who - after being sold into slavery by his jealous brothers - ended up becoming second in command in Egypt. God used this Joseph to store up grain in Egypt, thus saving many lives during a seven-year famine.

Now, toward the end of the story, Joseph has his father and brothers move from their home in Canaan to a region in Egypt called Goshen.

Genesis chapter 47 tells about the famine's severity, despite all the grain Joseph had saved. Egypt and Canaan wasted away because of the famine. The Egyptians were selling their livestock, land and even themselves as servants to the king (called a Pharaoh) for food.

Not exactly a pretty picture.

But Joseph's family (who were called Israelites) settled in Goshen, where life seemed pretty good by comparison. Four hundred years later, Moses would lead the Israelites out of Egypt to the land that God promised them, but at this point in time Goshen was a place to live and grow.

"They acquired property there and were fruitful and increased greatly in number," the Bible says.

Today as I look around and see all the stress and despair in the world, I feel like I'm living in Goshen. That doesn't mean I don't have struggles and challenges. But every day, God supplies me with the peace and comfort I need. He feeds my soul and gives me strength.

And strength is a much-needed commodity.

Recently, a friend and I were talking about the discouraging reports when I started thinking about Psalm 91.

Oh, how I love this Psalm. I love to read it and let it soak into my soul.

Take this verse for example:

"He who dwells in the shelter of the Most High will rest in the shadow of the almighty."

By turning to God we can find shelter and shade even in the heat of turmoil.

Or this verse:

"If you make the Most High your dwelling ... then no harm will befall you, no disaster will come near your tent."

Or these verses:

"'Because he loves me," says the Lord, "I will rescue him; I will protect him, for he acknowledges my name.

"He will call upon me, and I will answer him; I will be with him in times of trouble, I will deliver him and honor him.

"With long life will I satisfy him and show him my salvation.'"

Tired of wasting away? I know the feeling, but I believe someday we'll be in our Promised Land - heaven. In the meantime, we can live in our own Goshen - maybe not a perfect place, but a place to live and grow.

Anyone can find his way to Goshen.

My journey began long ago. Back then I already believed that Jesus had died on the cross to save me from my sins and rose again.

So I asked God to forgive me for the things I'd done wrong (nobody's perfect) and to come into my heart. Slowly life began to change.

My journey has been a long one, filled with good times and bad, but God has never left me hopeless. He's always sent someone or something to help.

I'm sure there are other Christians who could tell you the same thing, who'd welcome you to accompany them on the same journey and to say:

"Welcome to Goshen."

God, Grace and Gladys Ellis

Never underestimate your grandma's prayers.

Ninety-year-old Gladys Ellis makes a habit of praying for her grandson, Brett, and his wife, Leeanna, before they travel from Fremont to her parents' home in Durant, Iowa.

"If we're ever going on a long road trip, she calls to let us know she's praying for us and that God will be with us and protect us on our way," Leeanna said.

Those prayers were especially appreciated on Dec. 20.

Brett and Leeanna were headed to Durant that day.

Before they left, the two checked road conditions via a computerized map from the Iowa Department of Transportation.

Road conditions seemed fine. So even though it had snowed in Fremont, the couple set out at 7 a.m.

Everything was all right until they reached Des Moines and a portion of Interstate 80 where it joins with I-35.

To get onto I-80 involves traveling on a big curve.

They were in the left-hand lane and had just passed a semi, when the back end of the car slid to the right and they were suddenly going sideways on the Interstate's curve.

Looking straight out the windshield they could see an embankment more than 100 feet down.

Brett remained calm, never saying a word. Leeanna braced herself and yelled, "Hold on!"

She thought for sure they were going over the embankment. And if that happened, she was certain the car would roll.

Even Brett was convinced they'd go into a ditch and was looking for a place that wasn't so steep as he tried to correct the car's direction.

Then he overcorrected and suddenly the car turned the other way - again traveling sideways.

He corrected again and the car was headed the right way once more.

"Brett was so proud of himself - that he got us out of a near accident - and I'm sitting there bawling my eyes out," Leeanna said. "The rest of the ride, we were pretty quiet."

When they reached her parents' home, Leeanna grabbed her mom and cried, because "I was just sure we weren't going to get to see her for Christmas."

Leeanna believes God protected them and she's still amazed at how calm her husband was.

"He's been in situations before where he's panicked and put a car in a ditch. When I told my mom that, she was convinced that it was the Lord protecting us," she said.

And maybe that's where Gladys' prayers come in.

Gladys prayed for God's protection. I believe he answered her prayer and gave Brett the grace and sense of calmness he needed - right when he needed it.

It reminds me of the Bible story in Exodus chapter 16. At this point, Moses has led the Israelites out of slavery in Egypt. They're in the desert and they're hungry.

So one morning, God sends bread, called manna, from heaven. Manna is white, looks like frost on the ground and tastes like wafers made with honey.

The Lord tells Moses to have the Israelites gather as much as they need, but nobody is supposed to keep any of it until morning.

Those who do that find that it stinks and has maggots in it the next day. The only exception is when the Israelites are told to gather twice as much the sixth day - because on the seventh day, they're simply supposed to rest.

For 40 years, God provides manna. The Israelites get enough just for each day - a continual reminder of their dependence on God.

Christian author Beth Moore shares a modern-day manna lesson in her wonderful DVD/workbook series, "A Woman's Heart: God's Dwelling Place."*

In it, she tells how distraught she was when her friend's 4-year-old child died of leukemia. Moore, the mother of two daughters, cried out to God, telling him that she just couldn't live if something like that happened to her.

Then God led her to the manna story.

"He was telling me that a sufficient amount of mercy and grace would be set aside for me every day of my life, enough every morning," she writes.

In the DVD lesson, Moore talks about sobbing at the child's funeral. Then she noticed the grace that seemed to carry the child's mother. And God spoke to Moore's heart: "My grace, Beth, is given according to need. The reason you look on another situation and think 'I could never bear that if I were them,' is because you don't have that present portion of grace - because you don't need it - and when you do, it will be there for you - as long as you gather it."

Moore explained that while God provided the manna, the Israelites still had to leave their tents and gather it.

In the same way, God provides us the grace we need, day by day. But we can't just sit in our slump and do nothing. We need to seek God. Moore says that means taking all our emotional stuff - our anger, temptation or whatever - to God to be treated daily by his "manna."

Now I've never lost a child or had my car slide down an Interstate sideways, but I know what it is to fear losing a loved one.

And somehow the stories of Gladys and manna from heaven help me to trust God a little more - and show me that I don't need to be afraid.

That no matter what happens he will give me that day-by-day grace to handle it - just when I need it.

*Used by permission of Lifeway Christian Resources

The God Who Fights for Us

As a kid, I was picked on pretty much all through school.

I grew up being called painful names like "dog" and "frog" and "goofy."

In fourth grade, I didn't even want to see the sun rise because it meant I had to go to school. In eighth grade, my grades plummeted as I spent almost every moment trying to avoid two girls determined to beat me up - probably because I was different.

I answered too many questions in class. I had messy hair and unstylish clothes.

While still in elementary school, I told my mom that I was getting picked on. Mom said she would pray for me, but I couldn't imagine how her prayers would help. Obviously she didn't understand the seriousness of the situation.

Later on in life, I told myself that I'd used my brains to stay out of fights. Now that I am older I appreciate my mother's prayers and I know God protected me.

The whole situation reminds me of Moses and Israelites at the Red Sea. In this account, God used a man named, Moses, to lead the Israelites out of slavery in Egypt.

Exodus chapters 13 and 14 in the Bible tell about the Lord going ahead of them in a pillar of cloud by day and a pillar of fire by night.

But after the Israelites left Egypt, the Pharaoh and his officials realized they'd lost all these people's services and decided to pursue them.

By then, the Israelites were at the Red Sea. They looked up and saw the Egyptian army coming after them.

They just knew they were going to die.

But Moses knew better.

"Do not be afraid," he told the people. "Stand firm and you will see the deliverance the Lord will bring you today. The Egyptians you see today you will never see again. The Lord will fight for you; you need only to be still."

God told Moses to have the Israelites move on. He then had Moses raise his staff and stretch out his hand over the water.

The angel of God who'd been traveling with the Israelites, went behind them. And the pillar of cloud stood between them and the Egyptians.

"Throughout the night the cloud brought darkness to the one side and light to the other side; so neither went near the other all night long."

As Moses stretched out his hand, God drove the sea back with a strong east wind. The waters divided and the Israelites crossed on dry ground with walls of water to their right and to their left.

The Egyptians followed them, but God threw their army into confusion and made the wheels of their chariots fall off. God then made the water go back in its place. Water swept over the Egyptians and they all died.

Don't get me wrong. I'm not advocating that we kill those who pick on us, but I think there are times when fear, shame and despair can seem as overpowering as that army.

That's when we need to remember God's protection.

If you remember nothing else from this column, remember this: We have a God who will fight for us.

I love the thought of God putting a pillar of cloud and his angel between the Israelites and the Egyptian army. I love how he opened a way through the water where there seemed to be no way. And I love how he protected the Israelites from people who didn't just threaten to beat them up, but intended to kill many of them and take the rest back as slaves.

Today, we don't have to be enslaved by our fears. We need to stand firm, pray and trust in God's deliverance.

And can I tell you something?

While I didn't have many friends throughout my early years, God blessed me with good friends when I got to Midland Lutheran College. My pals, Martha Hartman and Deb Rector, and I have been friends for 30 years now.

Since college, God has blessed me with many other friends: Nancy and Doreen, who are surely better friends than I ever deserve (I never remember their birthdays and anniversaries like they remember mine) and Kandy and Jody who are a constant source of encouragement for my column writing.

I don't know what happened to those girls from eighth grade, but I figure they must have had bad lives to act the way they did. I pray that God will bless them and that they will come to know him.

And just as God told Moses to have the Israelites to move on, we, too, must move past the hurts and rejections in our lives.

Eventually, the Israelites would move into the land that God promised to their ancestors. Their Promised Land.

The Israelites had to leave their past behind.

And so should we.

Faith Muscles

I still remember where I was when I heard the news.

A longtime friend of mine had been in a terrible accident. He'd been thrown from his vehicle out onto hard highway pavement. He was in the hospital. No one knew for sure how he was.

I felt a hand on my shoulder as I started to choke up.

I began to pray that God would protect him, totally heal and restore him. I continued to pray as I went on my daily tasks, asking God to preserve the life of a friend who'd seen me through some tough years.

And God was faithful. Even today, I marvel at how well my friend survived that accident. I think he had a concussion and he was skinned up pretty badly.

But he didn't have one broken bone.

It was truly a miracle.

During his recovery, he shared with me two things the doctor said helped him.

First, my friend was in great shape. He exercised all the time. That exercise built up muscles that helped withstand the impact when he hit the pavement. Secondly, he was wearing a good leather coat. That coat was a mess after the accident, but it helped shield him from being scraped up any more badly than he was.

My friend has long since recovered, but he taught me a lesson that I carry to this day.

When I think of my friend, I think of how much his built-up muscles remind me of faith.

To me, faith is a muscle that must be exercised or it atrophies. I truly believe we exercise it when we pray, seek God's will through Bible reading and trust him to get us through all the difficult - and even not so difficult - times in our lives. We feed that faith muscle when we attend church and hear the miracle stories of fellow believers.

And just as my friend's built-up muscles withstood the force of the impact, I believe our faith serves as a cushion when we hit those very hard times in life.

Just like that heavy leather coat kept him from being banged up any worse than he was, I believe faith serves as a shield for us.

The Bible even seems to support my theory.

In the New Testament book of Ephesians, chapter 6, starting with verse 10, the Apostle Paul urges his readers to be strong in the faith. And he urges them to do something else: to put on the full armor of God.

He compares our protection against life's battles and our enemy, Satan, to a suit of armor.

Among those pieces is the shield of faith. With this shield, Paul says we can "extinguish all the flaming arrows of the evil one."

I honestly believe that just as we have a loving God who is always on our side, there is an evil one who hurls swift arrows of fear, doubt, despair and other awful things at us.

That's when we need to hold up that shield of faith so those things can bounce off of us.

How do we do that?

I believe when red, hot fear comes at us like a flaming arrow, we need to pray to God to give us peace. We need to remember and even repeatedly say aloud one of God's comforting Scriptures like: "For God has not given us a spirit of fear, but of power and of love and of a sound mind." 2 Timothy 1:7.

Or "What time I am afraid, I will trust in the Lord." Psalm 56:3.

Or the second part of 1 John 4:4 "greater is he that is in you, than he that is in the world" - meaning the Holy Spirit who is in you is greater (more powerful) than the evil one who is in the world.

And when we face a tough situation, I like, "I can do all things through Christ who strengthens me." Philippians 4:13.

I've written Bible verses on scraps of paper or index cards and re-read them daily until I could say them without even looking. I've read the Bible and attended church enough throughout the years so that some verses just come to mind. And the Bible even talks about the Holy Spirit bringing God's teaching to our mind.

I hate to think what would have happened if I'd been in an accident like my friend. With my flabby physical condition, I probably would have had many broken bones. I wouldn't have had those built-up muscles.

But spiritually, I believe my faith muscles could have pulled me through.

Much more than that, our strong and loving God can bring us out of the toughest accident, the darkness night, the deepest pit.

To my dear friend, who has been so good to my husband, Chuck, and I throughout the years, I pray that God will bless you in innumerable ways and that many good things will happen to you in the future. You deserve it.

And for those of you who think you may be in poor spiritual shape, I have two words:

Start exercising!

Wrestling with God

If everything always goes perfectly at your job, then maybe you can't relate to what I'm going to tell you.

But if you're like most people, you have days or weeks when things at work don't go so smoothly.

Most of the time, my job goes very well, but I had one of those less-pleasant weeks a few years ago.

It happened while my boss was on vacation and I was in charge. We had computer problems and personnel issues. We missed deadlines.

I was up to my ears in frustration.

So I took a little walk and ended up having a wrestling match with God.

During the walk, I told God my troubles and asked why he'd put me in that situation.

Then God spoke into my spirit.

It wasn't with audible words. It was more like a deep impression or thought in my heart and soul.

But I knew it was from God.

The words were:

"Lean on me."

Something else happened during that walk. I was reminded of a story about a Biblical wrestling match.

I looked it up when I got home later.

And smiled.

The Bible story, found in Genesis chapter 32, involves a man named Jacob. Now Jacob was a crafty character who cheated his own brother, Esau, out of the inheritance and blessing that normally went to the first-born child in those days.

That trick sent Jacob fleeing for his life from a sibling who wanted to kill him. Jacob traveled far away to another place where he married two sisters and became the father of 12 sons.

Eventually, however, Jacob wanted to go home. So he started out with his large family. But on the way, Jacob learned that his brother and 400 men were coming to meet him.

Fearing that his family would be killed, he divided them into two groups. If one group was murdered, perhaps the other could escape.

Then he prayed fervently.

What happened next amazes me. Jacob sent his family groups across a stream and was all alone.

Well ... until a man showed up.

Who was this guy? Many believe he was a pre-incarnate appearance of Christ and others say he was an angel.

At any rate, he began to wrestle with Jacob.

They wrestled all night, then the man touched the socket of Jacob's hip, disabling it and causing him to limp. The man wanted Jacob to let him go. But Jacob wouldn't. Instead, the same guy who wanted a blessing so badly that he stole one from his own brother, now wanted another one.

I wonder if Jacob's heart ached for years knowing that the beautiful words of his father's blessing were meant for someone else. Maybe this time, Jacob wanted a blessing that was truly all his own.

But instead of an immediate blessing, the man had a question.

"What is your name?" he asked.

So Jacob told him.

To understand the significance of this you have to know that the name, Jacob, means "deceiver" and "supplanter."

Jacob had really lived up to his name.

But he would get a new one.

"Your name will no longer be Jacob, but Israel because you have struggled with God and with men and have overcome."

I still remember reading that after my very long day. It's funny, but those last words seemed to jump right off the page and into my heart.

I think God was showing me - that with his help - I'd already overcome many struggles and that he'd get me through the rest.

By the way, the man did bless Jacob who had a successful meeting with his brother.

Yet Jacob never lost his limp. I've read where the limp was a reminder that Jacob should never rely on his own strength, but on God's.

I picture Jacob leaning on a stick to keep his balance as his limped through the rest of his life.

I don't know if that's so, but one thing is certain:

I know he had to lean on God.

And that's just what God told me to do years ago on that walk.

My Art Teacher and the Fiery Furnace

My poor art teacher.

After all these years, I still kind of feel sorry for her.

It happened in my college jewelry making class. I started to put a piece in the kiln, but was only using oven mitts.

My teacher nearly went into a meltdown - not out of anger, but terror.

Didn't I know I was supposed to use the metal tongs as well?

Oops. I was behind in my reading. I hadn't gotten to that chapter in the textbook.

I quickly put down the item and got the tongs. In the meantime a foreign exchange student in my class found the situation hilarious.

"Ho, ho, ho," he said, almost sounding like Santa. "You stick your hand in the fire!"

Nothing like entertaining the troops.

Now as you probably know, there's great Bible story about three guys who were facing a really hot situation.

It occurs after Babylonian King Nebuchadnezzar has taken many Israelites captive. Among them are three men, Hananiah, Mishael and Azariah.

We know them better by their Babylonian names: Shadrach, Meshach and Abednego.

As the story goes, the king has built a 90-foot-tall gold statue, which he orders everyone bow down and worship.

Those who don't will be thrown into a fiery furnace.

Guess who won't bow down? Yep, those three stubborn Israelites. And when brought before an enraged king, they even say "If we are thrown into the blazing furnace, the God we serve is able to save us from it, and he will rescue us from your hand, O king."

Then our non-compromising friends say something that I consider the epitome of God-fueled faith.

Immediately after making their first statement, they follow up with: "But even if he does not (rescue us), we want you to know, O king, that we will not serve your gods or worship the image of gold you have set up."

Did you catch that phrase "even if he does not...."

How many of us can say, "Even if God never heals me on this earth, I will remain faithful"?

"Even if God never brings along that mate I've prayed for so long...."

"Even if God never lets me have a child...."

"Even if....."

The king doesn't take this response very well.

And from a management point of view, why should he? Weren't they being insubordinate? And if he let them get away with not bowing down, what's to keep others from refusing to follow his orders?

But this king is about to see something he won't forget.

He orders the furnace heated seven times hotter than normal. (Did you know that "seven" is God's number of completion and perfection? I can just imagine God cooking up the perfect lesson.)

Next, the king has some of his strongest soldiers tie up the three men and throw them into the furnace. The furnace is so hot that it kills the soldiers. So you'd think our three friends would be gone, right?

Suddenly, the king leaps to his feet.

"Weren't there three men we tied up and threw into the fire?" he asks.

Everyone agrees that the king's math is correct.

"Look," he says, "I see four men walking around in the fire, unbound and unharmed, and the fourth looks like a son of the gods!"

The king orders our three fellows to come out of the fire, which they do. They're not hurt, their clothes aren't scorched - and they don't even smell like smoke.

What's more, the ropes - or whatever was used to tie them - were gone. Which makes me wonder: Does it sometimes take a fiery trial to burn off the ropes of doubt, fear or regret - things that have us all tied up? Then after we've been through the fire, we know we can trust our God to get us through anything.

We don't like those furnace times - the times we hear about layoffs at work; or that our loved one was in a bad accident; or that the doctor wants us to come back because something on our test doesn't look quite right.

Suddenly, we can start to feel our faith evaporating faster than the sweat on our brow. But it's at these times that we have to remember who's with us in the furnace. Bible scholars tell us that the fourth man in the furnace could have been an angel or the pre-incarnate manifestation of Christ. Either way, those boys weren't alone.

And neither are we.

I'm reminded of that when I think about the time I had a routine medical test and was called back for an ultrasound due to a perceived abnormality.

I remember going to a birthday lunch for a friend after I got the news. Sitting across from me was a woman, bouncing a grandchild in her lap. I thought how I'd like to be a grandmother someday - and suddenly I wondered if I'd have the chance. I prayed and so did people from my church, then I went back for the ultrasound.

The "something" that specialists had seen earlier turned out to be nothing to worry about. And even today, I wonder if God miraculously healed that "something" in response to our prayers. I don't know if I'll ever find out on this side of the sky.

I do know, however, that God is faithful and he has protected me throughout my life - even when I tried to put an art project into a kiln without using tongs.

By the way, my art teacher recovered from her shock and I passed the class.

Isn't our God a real gem?

Elijah the Ancient Risk-Taker

Years ago, I learned a valuable lesson about taking risks.

It began while I was still in high school. I'd had a so-called friend who played what I considered a cruel joke on me. So by the time I got to college, I was a little wary of people.

Could I trust these new folks? I wasn't sure.

The thought was weighing heavily on my mind when I walked into the student union - a place on campus where we went to study and maybe eat a snack. While there, I noticed an older student sitting at a booth. From what I understood, the guy was a Vietnam veteran taking college classes.

We struck up a conversation.

I can't remember what I said.

But I remember what he said.

He basically told me that I had a choice to make. I could protect myself and never really get close to anyone. That way I wouldn't get hurt again.

Or I could take the risk of getting close to others. I might get hurt, but I could also form some wonderful friendships.

It didn't take me long to decide. I wanted warm, close friendships. I didn't want to be closed off from others.

I left the student union feeling as if a huge burden had been lifted from my heart. I could feel the smile on my face as I went back to the dormitory.

And guess what? During my college years, I made some great friends - two of whom have been my close pals for more than 30 years.

It was definitely worth the risk.

Now, the Bible has plenty of stories about risk-takers - those people who stepped out in faith and then saw the miraculous.

One of my favorites is a man named Elijah.

Oh my, he was a gutsy guy.

Telling wicked King Ahab that God wasn't going to send rain to Israel for a few years.

Asking God to send down fire from heaven to show the Israelites who the real God on the block was.

Having the Israelites kill the evil, false prophets of Baal.

Please don't misunderstand. Elijah wasn't some foolhardy daredevil. I believe he operated out of God-fueled - and God-guided - courage.

But somewhere along the line, Elijah's courage faltered. After the prophets of Baal were killed, evil Queen Jezebel planned to have Elijah murdered.

Elijah got scared and ran away, eventually reaching Horeb, the mountain of God. There, Elijah went into a cave to spend the night. He probably didn't expect to have a chat with God, but the Lord asked Elijah why he was there. The discouraged prophet told how hard he'd worked for the Lord and how the people had rejected God's ways.

And as if the Lord didn't already know, Elijah said the people had murdered good, God-fearing prophets.

"I am the only one left and now they are trying to kill me, too," Elijah said.

That statement makes me sad.

Elijah must have felt so alone.

But he wasn't alone.

He had the God of the universe on his side.

God told Elijah to stand on the mountain, because the Lord was going to pass by.

Suddenly a great and powerful wind "tore the mountains apart and shattered the rocks before the Lord.

"But the Lord was not in the wind."

Then there was an earthquake. But the Lord was not in the earthquake. Then there was a fire, but the Lord was not in the fire.

"After the fire came a gentle whisper. When Elijah heard it, he pulled his cloak over his face and went out and stood at the mouth of the cave," the Scriptures say.

Once again, God asked Elijah what he was doing at Mount Horeb. Once again, Elijah shared his story.

But God had a plan. God basically told Elijah that the bad guys would be dealt with.

And Elijah would get a friend. That man was Elisha, who also would become a great prophet. (Yes, the two men have similar names.)

Anyway, Elijah went back, got Elisha and the two went on to serve the Lord.

As I read this story, it reminds me how powerful God is. If God can make a wind that tears mountains apart, plus an earthquake and fire, what do you think he can do for us?

Then, God shows his tender mercy. In a gentle whisper, he reminds us that we don't need to hide in the dark caves of fear and loneliness.

You know, Elijah could have decided to disobey - and not trust God - and to go back into that cave.

Why should he have taken the risk, especially with mean Queen Jezebel on the prowl?

But had Elijah stayed in that cave, he might never have met Elisha. Or been whisked away to heaven in chariot of fire. Or become the example that he is to us today.

Now, I'm not saying we should take foolish risks. You don't get married, quit a job or make a big financial investment on a whim.

Or even a whim and a half.

That's just not smart. We need to pray, read the Bible and ask God for direction - before making decisions. It also can be good idea to seek the advice of people we know as being Godly and devoted followers of Christ.

Then, when we know what we should do, we need to ask God to help us - and take those steps of faith.

I don't know where that man who gave me such good advice stood with God, but I believe the Lord put him in the right place, at the right time, to help a young woman have the courage to reach out to others after being hurt.

And as gentle as a whisper, God still guides me.

Lessons from Naaman

Someone once jokingly said that every story in the Bible is my favorite.

But really, one of my favorites is about a man named Naaman. As with other Bible stories, I like it because of all the lessons I see in it.

The story begins in the Old Testament book of 2 Kings starting with chapter 5.

In this account, Naaman was the commander of an army for the King of Aram. Naaman was a valiant soldier and highly regarded.

There was just one problem. He had leprosy, a terrible skin disease that was incurable in ancient days.

But Naaman had an uncommon advocate. She was a slave girl from Israel.

Now here are some lessons I've learned from this story:

*** Show compassion even to those who aren't necessarily compassionate toward you.** This girl, who was taken captive and forced into slavery, could have been bitter. But demonstrating Godly character, she chose to get involved. She enthusiastically recommended that Naaman go see a prophet named Elisha for help. So Naaman asked his king for permission. The king agreed, even sending a letter to the Israelite ruler, requesting that Naaman be healed.

*** Don't assume the worst**. When the Israelite king got the letter, he freaked out.

"Am I God? Can I kill and bring back to life? Why does this fellow send someone to me to be cured of his leprosy? See how he's trying to pick a quarrel with me."

The Israelite king automatically assumed that the other king had an evil agenda, which wasn't the case.

*** Sometimes things don't turn out the way we expect.** When Elisha heard what happened he had Naaman sent to him.

Naaman went with all his horses and chariots to see the prophet. It was probably a flashy caravan for those days.

But Elisha didn't even come out of his house. Instead, he had a messenger tell Naaman to wash seven times in the Jordan river.

Doesn't sound very mannerly does it? And Naaman didn't take it well. He went away angry and said, "I thought that he would surely come out to me and stand and call on the name of the Lord his God, wave his hand over the spot and cure me of my leprosy."

*** Listen to good advice even when you're in a bad mood.** At this point, Naaman's servants tried to reason with him. Wouldn't he have done some great deed if Elisha had asked him to? (You notice that Elisha didn't tell Naaman to climb the highest mountain or hog-tie a camel.)

So, the servants wondered, if all Elisha asked him to do was wash in the river, why didn't he do it?

*** Put your pride aside - and obey God**. It was probably a humbling act for a great commander, but Naaman dipped himself seven times in the muddy Jordan river. And God healed him. The Bible says that Naaman's "flesh was restored and became clean like that of a young boy."

Wow. And I thought Dove dishwashing detergent did a great job.

Anyway, Naaman went back to thank Elisha - who wouldn't accept any payment or gifts from the now-happy army commander. And why should he? God's miracles aren't for sale and the gift he gave to Naaman was priceless.

*** Remember that helping people can change their lives.** After he was healed, Naaman said he wouldn't worship any other god. And Naaman asked that God would forgive him whenever he had to accompany his own boss into a temple where people worshipped a false god.

It was obvious that Naaman's transformation was more than skin deep. Which perhaps shows that even more than being healed physically, Naaman needed to experience the power and mercy of the one true God.

As I read this story, I'm reminded of how creative God is. He doesn't have just one way of doing things. He had Naaman dip seven times in a river. Jesus put mud on a blind man's eyes to heal him and simply told a paralyzed man to get up and walk - and he did.

Years ago, one of my neighbors said she'd quit asking God to solve a problem a certain way. She'd just pray: "God please work this out - and let me know what you decide."

That takes faith, but I think it's about the smartest way to pray I've ever heard of. While I may think there's only one way to resolve a difficult situation, I've watched God come up with better - and usually easier - ways to work things out.

Oh - a couple more thoughts. I think Naaman's story also shows that:

* No situation is hopeless.

* Sometimes we have to go the extra mile to see results.

* And being told to go jump in the lake (or river) isn't necessarily a bad thing.

God and Chuck's Cars

He sits in front of the computer just dreaming.

Page after Web page, he gazes at rusted out old bodies of cars and trucks parked in weed-filled junkyards.

It boggles my mind.

But to my husband, Chuck, they're not just yesterday's leftovers - they're tomorrow's possibilities.

Just the other night I watched as Chuck offered a heavy sigh while he looked at the picture of a 1955 Chevy.

It was just a shell if even that. No front end. No doors or trunk lid.

Then there was the Jeep Wagoneer. Its flat tires looked almost comical. And what little paint the thing had only seemed to keep the vehicle from totally being covered in rust.

I'd be remiss in not mentioning the Olds Cutlass.

Now, I'll bet this was a nice car at one time. But minus the motor and tires, it looked like another worthless hunk of junk.

After a very short time, I had to ask: "Why do you spend so much time looking at these things?"

I should have known better.

"I don't see a rusted out car," Chuck said. "I see a nice interior. I see paint that's so glossy it looks like you could see a mile into it - and chrome wheels. I hear the rumble of a stout motor."

Honestly, I'm not making this up. My quiet, man-of-few-words husband said all that.

And he went on.

"I see the finished product," he said. "Go to any car show and you'll see many cars in similar conditions that have been transformed through hard work, time and money."

Oh. He said the "M" word.

Money. It can take more than a good chunk of change to transform these beasts into beauties.

I sat quietly as Chuck pulled up photographs of beautifully restored cars and trucks.

There was the 1948 orange and silver, five-window Chevy pickup. Next, Chuck showed me a 1970 Olds Cutlass. It was bright orange, had a black stripe and factory style mag wheels.

And then there was that 1955 yellow and white Chevy. It had wide, white-wall tires and shiny tri-bar hubcabs.

Yep. It was pretty and a far cry from the rusted out junkyard version I'd seen earlier.

I guess Chuck had a point. Although I don't know when we'd ever get the money to restore vehicles like that I can admire the work on cars and trucks that have undergone such dramatic transformations.

And I have to acknowledge people who will spend the time and money to restore a vehicle, which someone like me would see as being beyond hope and not worth the work.

Perhaps here is where Chuck sees an analogy that touches one of the deepest places in my heart.

"A lot of times, we as Christians want our pastor or someone else to do the transformation," Chuck said. "We want to sit back and revel in the finished product when we need to be the ones putting the time, effort and money into touching and affecting the lives of other people around us - because a life transformed through Jesus Christ is worth more than any car will ever be."

I think Chuck is right and his words remind me of several Bible stories.

When Jesus looked at people with leprosy, do you think he only saw the disease - or the whole and healthy people they could become?

Did he only see a short, despised tax collector named Zacchaeus - or did he see a man of God in the making?

And after Christ rose from the dead and ascended into heaven, do you think he saw a man called Saul of Tarsus, who was persecuting Christians, and said: "This guy is hopeless"?

No. I don't either.

Thank goodness. If Christ had given up on that troublemaker, he never would have become the man we know today as the Apostle Paul, who went on to write some of the most beautiful words I've ever read.

Toward the end of his life, Paul wrote: "I have fought the good fight, I have finished the race, I have kept the faith. Now there is in store for me the crown of righteousness, which the Lord, the righteous judge, will award to me on that day - and not only to me, but also to all those who have longed for his appearing."

Did you catch that phrase: "finished the race"?

Isn't that what we all want to do? We want to cross the finish line as a winner. Yet who among us can't look back on our own lives and see some rust, some dents, a flat tire?

So isn't it great that where we see blemishes, bulges and bad hair, Christ sees the eternal beauty of a soul redeemed?

I wonder what would happen if we started looking at each other more that way.

If we prayed a little more for one another.

If we hoped a little more. Gave a little more.

And if we saw people the way that Chuck sees cars.

You know, I'm starting to think that those old cars don't look so bad after all.

Maybe there is a little potential.

The Best Stain Remover

I got a stupid bloody nose the other day.

I was frustrated because it happened in the morning while I was getting ready for work. Worse yet, I got some blood on my favorite sweatshirt - a particularly warm one that I like to wear to bed and also outside on a cold day. I quickly stuck my shirt under cold water to get out the little stains.

It looked like I'd succeeded until I held it up to the light.

There were still small stains and I wondered if I'd ever get them out.

I was thinking about those stains when - out of curiosity - I decided to call Cammi Strong.

Cammi is the forensic lab manager for the Nebraska State Patrol Crime Lab in Lincoln.

About two years ago, I interviewed her when I wrote a package of stories about those behind-the-scenes people who help sexual assault victims. We talked about DNA and its use in evidence.

This time, I wondered if she could detect blood even if it looked like it was gone.

She can.

"Sometimes the quantities are so minute that they can't be seen, but they're still detectable or present," she said.

Much of the time, in a case where someone has washed a stain off a wall or otherwise tried to clean away blood, an expert can use a chemical called Luminol.

"When you spray it on an area where a blood stain used to be, it glows," she said. "It's a very sensitive test and often used in crime scene analysis when they're trying to detect if the blood stains have been cleaned up."

Such things amaze me.

But in thinking about stains and a chemical that can detect them, I also can't help but think about the so-called stains we carry around inside us.

They're not blood stains, but they've colored our outlook on life.

That stain may be guilt over something we did years ago. It could be a past relationship or action that now shames us.

Or something cruel we said.

Or something we didn't do.

We may have asked God to forgive us years ago, but somehow forgiving ourselves seems harder. We may even forget about it for a while, then it surfaces in our memory like scum on a pond.

So we find ourselves telling God once more how sorry we are - and maybe wondering if he could forgive us at all.

Can I tell you that he can?

And does.

Take a look in the Scriptures.

In the New Testament book of 1 John, chapter 1, verse 7, it says that "the blood of Jesus Christ, God's son, cleanses us from all sin."

Not some.

Not a little.

But all.

Looking at my sweatshirt, I wouldn't think of blood as a cleansing agent. But Christ's sacrifice on the cross washes away every sin-stained aspect of our lives.

And what Christ cleans up is gone. Not even Cammi's Luminol could detect it, because it's just not there.

So why do we still keep acting like it is?

Maybe it's because we see things in human terms.

We know how hard it is for us to forgive others.

And because we have trouble forgiving, we assume that it must be just as difficult for God. But I think that's where we forget about God's patience and mercy.

Look at 1 John 1:9, which says: "If we confess our sins, he is faithful and just and will forgive us our sins and purify us from all unrighteousness."

Faithful and just.

Sounds like loyal and fair. Sounds like someone's who's on our side - who doesn't ride the waves of emotion when it comes to forgiving someone.

I really believe that we can trust God's word and that he will forgive us. So I've prayed, "Please forgive me God. And Lord, please help me to forgive myself and not dwell on the past."

Now, the Apostle Paul had one big crummy past. Before he became a servant of Christ, Paul was known as Saul of Tarsus. He persecuted Christians. He had them thrown into jail. He stood by and nodded his approval as people killed a Christian named Stephen.

After his conversion, Paul could have spent a lot of time wallowing in his past.

Instead, he looked ahead.

I'm not saying that he didn't regret what he did or ask forgiveness. But I've never read where Paul spent a lot of time mentally beating himself up for past mistakes.

He was too busy looking to the future. He had a job to do. He needed to tell others about Christ.

And maybe that's the approach we need to take. Instead of wasting time mourning over things we can't do anything about - if we truly can't do anything about them - maybe we need to ask God to help us keep our focus on him - on his goodness, his forgiveness and how we can share his love with others.

You might be pleased to know that I finally did get the blood out of my sweatshirt.

I was so happy. My shirt never looked so good.

There was just one little problem.

Somehow I managed to get a little blue ink on my sleeve.

Oh well.

This is one stain I can live with.

Straightening Up

Toward the end of her life, my mother, Evelyn, suffered terribly from osteoporosis and curvature of the spine.

Her bent appearance was heart-wrenching. She had to use her hand to hold up her head when she sat down - and then she just looked tired and worn.

Getting her to eat was a challenge.

I remember sitting with her one day. It took an hour and a half to get her to eat half a sandwich and two small dishes of ice cream. I assume swallowing wasn't very pleasant, not with her head bent down.

Her condition reminds me of a Bible story in which Jesus heals a woman who was bent over and couldn't straighten up at all.

The account is found in the 13th chapter of the book of Luke, starting with verse 10. In this story, it's the Sabbath and Jesus is teaching in the synagogue. The Scriptures say the woman has been crippled by a spirit for 18 years. When Jesus sees the woman, he calls her forward.

Some commentaries make note of this. Jesus called a woman forward in a culture that typically shunned females.

Jesus then tells her: "Woman, you are set free from your infirmity." He places his hands on her and immediately she straightens up and praises God.

Now, right away, a man known as the synagogue ruler is furious.

How could Jesus break the rules?

People are supposed to work six days a week. But on the Sabbath (which is kind of like our Sunday), they're not supposed to do anything. That's the rule. He smugly announces that the woman should have been healed on one of those other days.

Wrong thing to say.

Jesus refutes that man and those like him. I can almost hear the fury in Christ's voice as he calls them hypocrites and asks: "Doesn't each of you on the Sabbath untie his ox or donkey from the stall and lead it out to give it water? Then should not this woman, a daughter of Abraham, whom Satan has kept bound for 18 long years, be set free on the Sabbath day from what bound her?"

When Christ says this, his opponents are humiliated, but the people are delighted.

Today, I believe people look at these passages and concentrate on Christ's adversaries, so bent on trying to discredit Jesus that they expose their utter disregard for this poor woman.

But I'm drawn to the woman. Eighteen years is a long time.

I'm also reminded of Beth Moore's comments in her great DVD/ workbook series, "A Woman's Heart - God's Dwelling Place."*

In a video session, the Christian speaker and author seems to refer to being bent over - not physically - but spiritually, mentally and emotionally.

I think she's on to something.

While some people may look like they're standing tall, they're actually bent over inside - bent from carrying a heavy burden of guilt, shame, regret or despair. And they've been hunched over for so long that they don't know any other way to live.

Maybe that's when they - and we also - must remember how Jesus tenderly called the woman forward. Perhaps nobody else noticed the woman or her miserable circumstances, but Christ did. Then he spoke to her and even touched her.

And she was healed.

I wonder how many people today think nobody - not even God - notices their circumstances. And I wonder if they know that he's calling them forward, to come to him, to let him touch them and heal the hurt in their hearts.

The woman didn't have to come forward when Christ called. It certainly couldn't have been comfortable to walk up in front of the people in the synagogue - with all eyes on her. But maybe she was so tired of being hunched over that she was ready to try anything.

And when she took those steps of faith, the miraculous happened. She was healed. She could finally straighten up.

I wonder how different life looked to her after that. What was it like to be able to look people in the face? To look at something besides her feet and the ground? And to be able to just glance up and see the sun and the clouds and blue sky?

I also wonder how many of us are willing to seek God for help. It might not mean that our lives suddenly become perfect. We may still need to deal with the consequences of our past, to pay off debt or clean up a mess or work to restore relationships.

But with the healing power of God and continued dependence on him, what if we could stand up straight on the inside - no longer bent over under those heavy burdens.

I wonder.

My mother never did straighten up physically, but I love to imagine her walking to the throne of God. And as she does, I picture her gradually, beautifully straightening up before the Lord, looking into her savior's smiling face.

And I think how nice it must be for her to stand tall and see the sun.

*Used by permission of Lifeway Christian Resources.

Finding Jughead

It never fails.

Sometime between midnight and 2 a.m. our old dogs decide they must go outside and go to the bathroom.

Their habit has warranted my trying to go to bed early to compensate for my brief loss of sleep, but that doesn't always occur. At any rate, I can usually count on their synchronized bladders.

It happened again the other night. Two of our three pooches let me know they needed to make their midnight run. So I let them out, then called them in.

Funny thing. Our old beagle, Jughead, didn't go outside, but I couldn't find him anywhere in the house. Someone must have let him out earlier.

I called for him to no avail.

How typical. He hates to come in on cool nights when there's a slight breeze. I imagine his beagle nose is taking in all sorts of interesting smells that the rest of us can't begin to detect.

So I figured I'd leave him out a while longer and try again.

I settled into a recliner with a blanket.

But I couldn't doze off. After all, the dog is overweight and almost 12 years old. What if he had a heart attack or something?

Then the Bible story of the shepherd going after the lost sheep came to my mind.

You know the story. It's a parable - one of those stories Jesus told to help people understand how God operates. With everyday examples that ancient people understood, Jesus painted word pictures of the Lord and his kingdom. Very often, they are portraits of God's love.

The parable of the lost sheep is no different.

In this story, found in the book of Luke, chapter 15, a man has 100 sheep, but loses one. He leaves the 99 to find the one that has wandered away.

Can you imagine the shepherd, with his heart pounding, scanning the countryside, looking over ledges and into caves or even crossing a stream?

Anyway, the parable continues with the shepherd finding his lost sheep and being so overjoyed that he calls his friends and neighbors to celebrate.

"I tell you that in the same way there will be more rejoicing in heaven over one sinner who repents than over 99 righteous persons who do not need to repent," Jesus says.

It's a great story and with that thought in mind, I considered crawling out of the comfortable recliner to go hunting for Jughead.

But I didn't want to go after the "lost" beagle.

I just wanted to go back to sleep.

Then a thought hit me: Jesus never gets tired of going after the lost sheep.

God never gets tired - period.

Even the Biblical book of Isaiah chapter 40 says this: "Do you not know? Have you not heard? The Lord is the everlasting God, the creator of the ends of the earth. He will not grow tired or weary, and his understanding no one can fathom.

"He gives strength to the weary and increases the power of the weak..."

Looking back, I wish I'd remembered that last part of the verse as I pulled myself out of the chair and imagined looking around in a dark backyard - albeit fenced in - for a dog who's mostly black. I said a prayer and headed off.

Suddenly, I heard a familiar sound.

It was Jughead. He was at the back door.

I opened the door and he ran in like an excited, wiggly puppy looking for his treat. (You wonder why he's overweight? The dog has me trained very well.)

Anyway, we all settled down again to sleep. Yet I can't escape the thought of God's tenacious pursuit of us and what steps he takes - through songs, sermons, people and even newspaper columns - to draw us to Himself.

And I think about the times I've probably considered myself too tired, too busy or too something else to help point the way to a loving God.

In my kitchen, I have a small reprint of a painting by the late English artist Walter Hunt. I believe the painting is called "Found."

It depicts a collie that appears to have found a lost lamb in the snow.

The collie's head is tilted back and the dog seems to be barking to alert an unseen shepherd that the bedraggled, lost lamb has been found.

Sometimes I think we should be more like that collie, calling out to our unseen shepherd on behalf of those lambs - lost in a storm of trouble, heartache or despair.

I believe people did that for me.

And I never gave any of them a doggie treat.

Faith, Angels and Balaam's Donkey

I love stories about angels.

Christian author and speaker Joyce Meyer tells a wonderful story about a man who came to one of her conferences in Arizona. The man wasn't a believer, but attended with his wife. During the event, he started crying and shaking and saying, "Don't you see them?"

Afterward, he told his wife that he saw some very tall men follow Meyer out to the platform. They were dressed in white and he thought they were part of a choir.

But when Meyer got up to speak these extra tall men formed a semi circle around her and lifted swords.

I think it's safe to say these guys weren't Secret Service agents.

And needless to say, the man became a Christian that day.

I heard another great story while watching the documentary series "Against All Odds," produced by American Trademark Pictures.

The story takes place in a town in the northern part of Israel - long before the nation's founding in 1947. Very few Jewish people were there then.

One night, a group of Arab terrorists decided to kill everybody in the Jewish community of Pekiin. Everyone was asleep except the rabbi.

The terrorists went to one part of the town, but saw tall, robed figures, who they assumed to be guards.

So the terrorists went to another part, only to see the same thing.

Finally, they decided to go through a cemetery. But the very tall, robed figures were there, too.

This time they lifted flaming swords. The terrorists ran away screaming and dropping their weapons.

Alerted by the noise, the rabbi looked to see what had happened and saw the figures. The story has been passed down since then.

Do these accounts have any Biblical backing? I believe so, especially after I read stories like these:

Guarding the garden

Remember the story of Adam and Eve? They were cast out of the Garden of Eden after they ate the forbidden fruit.

Now look at Genesis 3:24: "After (God) drove the man out, he placed on the east side of the Garden of Eden cherubim and a flaming sword flashing back and forth...."

An angel and a talking donkey

I love the story of Balaam's donkey in the Bible.

Who's Balaam?

By most accounts, he was a Gentile who may once have been a true prophet, but then went astray. Or he may have been a false prophet from the start. Either way, he became involved in divination.

His story is found in the Old Testament book of Numbers, starting with chapter 22. In this account, the king of Moab wants to pay Balaam to put a curse on the Israelites.

God tells Balaam not to do that. Yet greedy Balaam keeps bugging God, who finally lets him go to the Moabite king.

Balaam saddles his donkey and takes off, but God isn't happy. So an angel of the Lord blocks the road. When the donkey sees the angel standing with a sword, the animal heads off into a field.

Balaam beats the donkey.

Poor donkey.

Twice more, the donkey tries to avoid the angel. One time, she presses close to a wall, crushing Balaam's foot against it. The last time - when there's no where else to turn - the poor donkey just lies down.

Each time, Balaam beats his donkey.

Then God lets the donkey have her say.

"What have I done to make you beat me these three times?" the donkey asks.

You'd think Balaam would be shocked to hear his donkey talk, but the guy's obviously too angry to think clearly.

"You've made a fool out of me! If I had a sword in my hand, I would kill you right now!" Balaam roars.

The donkey keeps a cool head.

"Have I been in a habit of doing this to you?" the donkey asks.

Balaam says no.

Then God opens Balaam's eyes and he sees the angel with the sword.

"The donkey saw me and turned away from me these three times," the angel says. "If she had not turned away, I would certainly have killed you by now, but I would have spared her."

In the end, Balaam blesses the Israelites three times - much to the Moabite king's chagrin. But Balaam isn't finished. In the New Testament book of Revelation, we read where Balaam taught the Moabite king to entice the Israelites into immorality.

Balaam later gets killed by an Israelite sword. His story, however, lives on, reminding us of the dangers of greed and disobedience to God.

So what happened to the donkey? I don't know. I hope she got to live a nice, long life - especially after putting up with Balaam.

As for angels, I do believe they exist today. I love the thought of God sending them to protect us. I pray that God always opens my eyes to his wonders.

And I hope I never get so far off track that God has to use an angel with a sword and a talking donkey to get me back on the right path.

Ankle Deep in Goop

You've got to love a good farm story.

And I think I have one. When I was a kid, my mom and I went to my uncle's farm.

Mom and her brother were going to talk so he suggested that my younger cousin take me to the barn to show me some kittens. We climbed into the hayloft where the kittens were, but the place was dark.

My cousin opened a door to bring in some light, but it wouldn't stay open. Trying to help, I looked down into the fenced-in lot below and saw two long boards near the base of the barn. If my cousin opened the door again, all I had to do was rest one of those long boards against it.

Surely then it would stay open.

So I hurried down to the lot. The ground looked solid although a bit cracked in some places. But as I stepped on it, my foot started to sink. I took another step and that foot sank, too.

I wasn't going to give up, though. I figured if I just made it to those boards I could stand on them.

But with every step my feet sank deeper and deeper, because under that deceptive and crusty brown layer was a gooey mixture of mud and cow manure.

Before long, I turned around and headed for more sturdy ground, but not before losing both of my shoes and my white knee socks in what seemed like a farmyard version of quicksand.

I made it out OK and I still remember my uncle laughing at my messy mistake.

He sent my cousin to find my shoes and socks.

Obviously the boy knew his way around the place much better than I did.

I still remember the wide smile on his face and his outstretched arms as he held up my muck-covered socks like the prize-winning catch of the day.

I never did get to see the kittens, but I learned something.

Appearances, even in a seemingly harmless place, can be deceiving.

At first glance, I thought I was going to be standing on solid ground, but I ended up ankle-deep in something I didn't want to be in.

Recently, I was sharing the humbling experience with my husband, Chuck, who reminded me of a Bible story about some other less-than-solid ground.

It's found in the New Testament book of Matthew in the Bible. In Chapter 7, Jesus is talking to the crowds. He says that everyone who listens to his words - and does what he says - is like a wise man who built his house on a rock. When the storms came, the house stayed intact because of its firm foundation.

But those who don't do what he says are like a foolish man who built his house on sand. When the storms came, his house collapsed. Why? It was built on shaky ground.

You don't have to be a Bible scholar to realize that Jesus and the word of God are the rock upon which we need to build our lives. That way we can withstand life's storms.

Those who build on other things, even things that seem good - like success, wealth or a great job - can face a big collapse when those things blow away like sand in bad, blustery storm.

How did I learn to build on the solid rock of Christ? I asked forgiveness of my sins and asked Jesus to come into my heart and be my Savior. I believed - and still believe - that he died on the cross to save me from my sins and rose again from the dead.

I pray, read my Bible and stay involved in church. I've asked God to help me love him with all my heart, soul, mind and strength and to love my neighbor as myself. I ask him to make me hungry for his word. I also seek out Christians, who are strong in the faith, so I can learn from them and hear how God has helped them in life.

Don't get me wrong. I'm no spiritual giant. I make plenty of mistakes. But I keep trusting that the Lord who started a good work in me isn't going to stop and that someday I'll be with him in heaven - the firmest ground there is.

That's good news for someone who really knows what it's like to walk in some stinky stuff here on earth.

You know, I don't think we even tried to salvage those socks.

The God Who Helps Us Fight Fear

Margaret Hillis knew fear.

She and her little children had stayed behind in a Chinese town as villagers fled advancing Japanese troops during World War II.

An American woman.

Far from home.

With untold numbers of fighters headed her way.

I try to picture myself in that situation.

Would I nervously glance toward a window, wondering if I'd see the face of an enemy? Would I try to push away thoughts of what battle-hardened soldiers might do to my precious children and me? Would I spend almost every minute praying for God's protection?

I can only imagine it.

But Margaret lived it.

I heard about missionaries Dick and Margaret Hillis one Sunday at church, when my pastor, the Rev. Mike Washburn, told their story.

I checked it out. It's from a book called "Steel in His Soul: The Dick Hillis Story" by Jan Winebrenner (The WinePress Group). I got permission to retell it.

The story begins when the couple were in China during the Japanese invasion.

They and their two children lived in the inland town of Shenkiu. Villagers there were fearful, because each day brought reports of the Japanese advance.

Then Dick developed appendicitis and knew his life depended on making a long journey by rickshaw to the hospital.

With deep foreboding, Margaret watched him leave on Jan. 15, 1941. Soon the Chinese colonel came with news. The enemy was near and townspeople must evacuate.

Margaret knew 1-year-old Johnny and 2-month-old Margaret Anne would never survive as refugees. So she stayed put.

"Early the next morning she tore the page from the wall calendar and read the new day's Scripture. It was Psalm 56:3 - 'What time I am afraid, I will trust in Thee (the Lord).'"

The town emptied that day.

The next morning Margaret arose, feeling abandoned. But the calendar's new verse was Psalm 9:10 - "Thou, Lord, hast not forsaken them that seek Thee."

"The following morning she awoke to distant sounds of gunfire and worried about food for her children. The calendar verse was Genesis 50:21 - 'I will nourish you and your little ones.' An old woman suddenly popped in with a pail of steaming goat's milk and another straggler arrived with a basket of eggs.

"Through the day, sounds of warfare grew louder and during the night Margaret prayed for deliverance. The next morning she tore the page from the calendar to read Psalm 56:9 - 'When I cry unto Thee, then shall my enemies turn back.'"

The battle loomed closer and Margaret didn't go to bed that night. Invasion seemed imminent. But the next morning, all was quiet.

"Suddenly, villagers began returning to their homes and the colonel knocked on the door. For some reason, he told her, the Japanese had withdrawn their troops. No one could understand it, but the danger had passed. They were safe. Margaret glanced at her wall calendar and felt she had been reading the handwriting of God!"

When I read Margaret's story, I'm reminded of the Bible verse, Zechariah 2:5, in the Old Testament which says "And I myself will be a wall of fire around it," declares the Lord, "and I will be the glory in her midst."

God is talking about Jerusalem, but I picture Margaret in that little town when I read that verse. I don't know if God protected Margaret with fire, but he guarded her. And each day, he showed her his glory.

Through simple verses on a calendar, God reminded Margaret that he knew her needs and hadn't abandoned her.

Margaret's husband, Dick, survived his medical emergency and went on to found what became Overseas Crusades International. The organization's Web site tells more of the Hillis story. Dick and Margaret eventually left China. They would have six children. Diagnosed with cancer in 1977, Margaret died just one week after their 45th wedding anniversary in 1981.

Dick later remarried and with his second wife, Ruth, visited China. Both lived to be in their nineties.

I believe all three are with the loving Lord who gave Margaret those Scriptures decades ago.

I also believe the Hillis story is an example of God's continual faithfulness and provision. Trusting God is a day-to-day walk of faith that includes prayer and Bible study. And hearing Margaret's story can help build our faith, too.

Because it's true that Margaret knew fear.

But more than that, Margaret knew God.

Jesus Is Our Glue

What do you think of when you think of glue?

Something that holds things together, right?

It makes me I think about when I was a student art teacher in the Fremont Public Schools system. The kids always had fun with glue and paste. One first-grader got glue in her hair. Others managed to get their sleeves in it. And some kids liked the sweet taste of that gloppy white paste - so I spent a lot of time saying things like, "Oh boys and girls, we're not going to eat our paste today are we?"

That was more than a couple of decades ago, but I thought about glue in a different way just the other night.

It happened after someone sent me a video* of a pastor named Louie Giglio, who was speaking at a concert. During his talk, Giglio said how wonderfully God has made human beings.

Then Giglio talked about a microbiologist who showed him the stuff we're really made of.

The microbiologist told Giglio about Laminin - the cell adhesion protein molecule. Laminin is what steel rods are when inserted into concrete - they hold it together.

Laminin is the glue that holds our cells together.

Next, Giglio showed a diagram and a photo of Laminin.

Guess what it looks like?

The glue that keeps us together is shaped like a cross.

I looked up Laminin on the Internet myself. And sure enough, there were diagrams and photographs showing this cross-shaped type of glue.

I guess I shouldn't be surprised.

Don't we see the fingerprints of God everywhere - in sunsets and flower-dotted fields and the spots on a giraffe? Why should we be surprised that God would leave his fingerprints inside of those he made in his own image? It's like a painter signing his name on a fine work of art.

I love the thought of having lots of little crosses inside me.

They point to the one who gave his life so we could live with him forever. They remind me that I'm his and that even on days when I think I'm going to come unglued - the Savior really is holding me together.

And the Scriptures would even support that.

One of the coolest parts of the video is when Giglio reads Colossians 1:17 from the Bible, which says: "He (Christ) is before all things, and in Him all things hold together."

Think your world is falling apart? Then turn to the one who really does have it all together.

Jesus is our glue.

As I look back on those days of student teaching, I remember how happy those kids were while working on their projects.

Ever watch little kids make artwork? Sometimes they almost get their noses right down to the paper when coloring a picture. They know which crayons they must use to make their drawings beautiful. And they fingerpaint with wild abandon.

I wonder if that's what it was like for God when he made the first human being. Did he get his nose right down to that clay as he formed the intricate parts of man's heart? Did he know just what colors he had to use to make the eyes and lips and freckles beautiful? And did he make hair with wild abandon?

You know, I never heard any little kid complaining that his project wasn't as pretty as someone else's or didn't turn out the way he wanted.

He was just thrilled. To him, his creation was terrific.

I wonder if that's what it was like for God. With the wisdom of the ages and the glee of a child, he formed the cells and sinews, muscles and bones of his masterpieces, the people for whom he would send his only son.

And to God, these works of art were - and still are - terrific.

* Video comes from a DVD called "How Great is Our God" by Louie Giglio.

Entering New Territory

You know the feeling.

You discover there's going to be a change in your job. Or in your personal life. Or in your health.

And suddenly you realize that life as you know it won't be the same.

You're headed into new territory.

And you're scared.

Maybe now is the time to read from the book of Joshua in the Bible.

Joshua was an aide to Moses.

You remember Moses - the guy who led the Israelites out of slavery in Egypt. The guy who raised his staff and the Red Sea parted.

Well, God did the parting, but Moses had a part to play.

Anyway, Moses did a lot of things, but he never actually got to shepherd the Israelites into the Promised Land.

He died before that.

Instead Joshua would be the one to lead the people into the land that God promised their forefathers.

What an opportunity.

Oh, but what a responsibility. Although he helped spy out the land 40 years earlier, Joshua had to know his life was going to change dramatically.

He was heading into new territory - in more ways than one.

I wonder if Joshua's heart pounded in his chest or his hands trembled. I think my insides would have been doing the jitterbug at the sight of the land in the distance.

But look at what God told Joshua: "Have I not commanded you? Be strong and courageous. Do not be terrified; do not be discouraged for the Lord your God will be with you wherever you go."

Some time ago, I was facing the possibility of changes in a

couple areas of my personal life. I remember the evening I realized that life as I knew it could change a lot. I knew I should just trust God to work everything out.

But at that point it seemed like I'd forgotten how.

"How am I supposed to trust you God?" I prayed. "Please don't tell me to do something, if you're not going to tell me how."

So he did.

That same night I attended a Beth Moore Bible study called "Believing God."* During this particular video session the Christian author and speaker talked about a time she was challenged to take her ministry a bit farther.

You know - into new territory.

She didn't want to do that and sobbed as she prayed. She was afraid she'd fail in her efforts and let God down.

Not long afterward, however, she went to hear another speaker. This woman couldn't have known what Beth was going through. But during that talk, the woman recited a Scripture in which the Lord says "I will not fail you."

Beth knew God was speaking to her heart - basically saying that while she might be afraid of failing God, he wouldn't fail her.

Later, she looked up the Greek word for "fail." One of the definitions means "a relaxing of the hand." So during the video, she demonstrated by gently gripping another woman's forearm and telling her to grip back.

The sight of their interlocked arms was powerful picture. It was a portrait of how God hangs onto us.

And how we need to hang onto him.

I began to think that while my trust level was low, I still knew one thing: I knew how to grip onto God and hold on for dear life.

And I knew if I held onto God, I would be OK.

How did I do that? I prayed whenever I could, especially if I felt a little fearful. I read the Scriptures and recited comforting verses to myself.

Some change did come.

Other things didn't change at all. But throughout all of it, God was faithful. He brought me the peace I needed - right when I needed it.

It's funny, but now I don't get so worried about things like I used to - even when I'm headed into new territory.

Because I know the Lord will be with me - wherever I go.

*Used by permission of Lifeway Christian Resources.

The Case of the Missing Purse

It happened the Tuesday before Thanksgiving last year.

I was headed to the grocery store to get a few things.

It was dark when I left work and after a few days of unseasonably warm weather the temperatures were beginning to drop that night.

I hurried into the store, bought my groceries and headed out. It was past 7 p.m. and I just wanted to get home. Out in the parking lot, I unloaded groceries into my car and was wheeling the cart to the drop-off site when a cold gust of wind chilled me. I hurried back to my car, drove home and pulled into my driveway.

Then I realized something.

I didn't have my purse.

I must have left it in the cart. Fear seized me and I was mad at myself, too. This wasn't the first time I'd left my purse in a cart and driven home. Twice (yes, twice) before, I done this in a hurry and some kind soul had taken my purse into the store. Both times had happened on summer days.

I just prayed another good person would help me this time, as well. But it was dark and right before the holiday. Gas prices were going up and people were caught in the financial crunch.

I reached the store and headed to the Customer Service Department.

No. Nobody had turned in a purse, but they'd take my name and phone number. A store manager tracked down a cart-pusher, but the boy hadn't noticed a purse either.

I tried to stay calm as I realized that my driver's license, credit card and the company cell phone were in my purse - my new purse. I went home and called the police. An officer came to the door and waited patiently as I called to cancel my credit/debit card. Next, I called my boss, who canceled the cell phone service and then I gave the ever-patient police officer information for his report.

The following day I went to the bank, then to the courthouse for a new driver's license. Everyone was so nice and sympathetic, but I felt terrible. I checked back with the grocery store.

No word on the purse.

I still prayed that I'd get my stuff back, but as days turned into weeks figured I'd been taught a good lesson. When our police reporter wrote a holiday safety story, he mentioned that women should keep their purses on their arms at all times and not leave them in a cart. I've followed that advice since.

Anyway, almost a year passed and the next thing I knew it was September. I was taking some time off when the phone rang one morning. An older gentleman was on the line. He told me his name, but for the life of me I can't remember it. He verified who I was and told me that his son was refurbishing a house in town. The older man was helping clean out the place when he found my driver's license and debit card in a drawer.

He figured I needed these things and wanted to bring them to me.

I was stunned.

He brought them to my house. He couldn't have known how long these items had been missing or that I'd already had replacements. He was very polite and I thanked him profusely. He didn't have to do this - but he chose to. And his action touched my heart.

After he left, I called the police department to report that two of the missing items were returned. The surprised-sounding dispatcher said this kind of thing rarely happens.

A couple days later the man called again and left a message on our phone.

Had I lost a cell phone, too?

The man left the cell phone in our mailbox. I took the phone back to work, where people were amazed by what had occurred.

Then one of the copy editors, Leeanna Ellis, pointed out a couple of things. The older man was a Good Samaritan - a person who went out of his way to help someone else. What's more, I had prayed to God that these items would be returned. And my prayer had been answered - a little differently and later than I expected - but answered just the same.

"You should write a Spiritual Spinach column about this," Leeanna said.

The idea sounded good at first, but then I wondered what I would write about. I'd already written a column about a Good Samaritan. Then my pastor, the Rev. Mike Washburn, pointed out the obvious.

Some people call it the Golden Rule. But many Christians know it as a verse from the New Testament book of Matthew, chapter 7, verse 12 which reads: "So in everything, do to others what you would have them do to you..."

One of my former Sunday School students, Natalie Murrish, said it best: "Treat other people the way you want to be treated."

My pastor mentioned that the man was doing just that. He probably would have wanted someone to return his lost things, so he brought mine back.

I don't know if this man goes to church or reads the Bible, but I know he lived what Jesus said to do in that verse.

As I think about the situation, I wonder how I treat others. Am I consistently kind? Do I make an extra effort to help others? How cheerfully do I give up extra time for someone else?

If God were to give me an exam, would I get a passing grade?

I can only hope so, but I can think of times when I'd score a low mark.

Someone once said that the great thing about God is that if you fail a test, he'll let you take it over and over until you pass it. I don't know if it works that way or not.

One thing I know: The do-good guy who brought back my stuff gets an "A" in my gradebook.

A Dark Night, A Faithful Friend

It had to be one of the darkest nights of my life.

I was a single mom and for longer than I could remember almost everything that could go wrong seemed like it did. Work was tough. Finances were tight and loneliness seemed to smother me like a hot blanket.

My son, Michael, was only about 2 years old that night. He had the flu. I had the flu. And we'd both been very sick. The toilet in the little house I rented was broken and overflowing and the landlord, who normally was very prompt with repairs, wasn't able to come over that night.

The house was dark. I was in bed. Michael was in bed in the next room crying. I knew I should get up and tend to him, but frankly I was so tired that I didn't have the energy to move.

Hot tears rolled down both sides of my face.

Then the thought came to me.

What did I have in my cupboards that I could take and end all this pain?

Funny thing. Almost as soon as that thought entered my mind, there was a knock at my back door. I maneuvered my way through the gloomy house.

It was my friend, Martha.

I'd met Martha years earlier. I was a college sophomore and she was a freshman. We were both taking psychology. It wasn't so hard for me, but Martha was struggling. Our professor announced one day that people who wanted to keep a good grade could do so by helping someone else. I'd been getting an "A" in the class, but then I had a bad grade on a quiz.

Out of pride I wanted to keep that "A" so I figured it wouldn't be so bad to help another person. The next thing I knew I was trying to help Martha remember psychological terms that sounded so similar, but meant different things. We quizzed in the dorm room. I shot questions at her one day when we went shopping for shoes.

It became fun.

And in the process Martha and I became friends.

I still remember the day that we took our final test for the class and Martha found out that she passed the course.

It felt good to watch her nearly skip all the way across campus and back to her dorm room. Our friendship continued and still today I hear her telling people about how I helped her get through psychology.

But what precious little I did for her has been repaid to me more times than I can count.

And that dark night so many years ago was just one example.

I opened the door and warned Martha that both Michael and I had the flu, but she didn't seem to mind.

She came in behind me as I plodded back to my bedroom. And in the dark, she began to tell me how worried she was about another friend of hers. That friend was dating a different guy and Martha was concerned that this fella just wasn't good for her. I listened quietly as she explained her reasons.

Before long, Martha apologized for bothering me and said she needed to get on her way. She hoped I'd be well soon. And she left.

By then Michael had stopped crying and had drifted off to sleep. I was so tired that I quickly dozed off, too.

The next day was another day. Plain and simple. The sun came out. Michael got up and so did I. Our toilet got fixed.

As time passed, I was amazed at how down in the dumps I'd gotten and what thoughts I'd had.

More than that, I was filled with gratitude to God. He brought me a friend at just the right time when I needed one the most. Martha and I have been pals for more than 30 years now. She was the maid of honor in my wedding. She's been a good friend - not only to me, but my husband, Chuck, and sons, Michael and Zachary.

The other night, Chuck and I were at a restaurant with Martha and many of her friends, who've become our friends. We had a good time and a lot of laughs. The whole thing reminds me of an Old Testament verse in the Bible. In the second half of Proverbs chapter 18, verse 24 it says "... there is a friend who sticks closer than a brother."

Martha is a friend like that to me. But as we all know, our dearest friend is Jesus, who is there every second of the day and night - even when our best friends can't be.

I would add that if you're going through a dark night of the soul like I did to please cry out to Christ and ask him to help you, then wait on him. Don't give up. You don't know what lies in the future.

Today's crisis can be tomorrow's gift.

And maybe someday, you'll be like me - not alone in the dark - but sitting among friends and loved ones and feeling enormously blessed.

Survival Scriptures

I call them "Survival Scriptures."

They're the ones you hang onto with both hands and a foot and your teeth, if necessary, to get you through life's turbulent times - or even when you begin to feel the ripples of a possible problem. They're the type of verses that you want to memorize or, at least, cut out and post someplace where you see them regularly.

I could provide a Top Ten list. But as many people know, God uses certain Scriptures to speak to us at various times.

So here they are, not listed in order of importance.

Because they're all important.

"Come to me, all you who are weary and burdened, and I will give you rest. Take my yoke upon you and learn from me, for I am gentle and humble in heart and you will find rest for your souls. For my yoke is easy and my burden is light." Matthew 11:28.

"Do not be anxious about anything, but in everything, by prayer and petition, with thanksgiving, present your requests to God and the peace of God which transcends all understanding will guard your hearts and your minds in Christ Jesus." Philippians 4:6-7.

"Those who wait upon the Lord shall renew their strength; They shall mount up with wings as eagles, They shall run and not be weary; They shall walk and not faint." Isaiah 40:31.

"Finally brothers, whatever is true, whatever is noble, whatever is right, whatever is pure, whatever is lovely, whatever is admirable; If anything is excellent or praiseworthy - think about such things." Philippians 4:8.

"...Fear not, for I have redeemed you; I have summoned you

by name; you are mine. When you pass through the waters, I will be with you; and when you pass through the rivers, they will not sweep over you. When you walk through the fire you will not be burned, the flames will not set you ablaze. For I am the Lord, your God, the Holy One of Israel, your Savior." Isaiah 43:1-3.

"And we know that all things work together for good to those who love God, to those who are called according to his purpose." Romans 8:28.

"For I know the plans I have for you, says the Lord of hosts, plans to prosper and not harm you. Plans to give you hope and a future. Then you will call upon me and come and pray to me and I will listen to you. And you will seek me and find me when you seek me with your whole heart." Jeremiah 29:1-13.

"Take delight in the Lord and he shall give you the desires of your heart." Psalm 37:4.

"I can do all things through Christ who strengthens me." Philippians 4:13.

"Trust in the Lord with all your heart and lean not on your own understanding; in all your ways acknowledge him, and he will make your paths straight." Proverbs 3:5-6.

"For God has not given us a spirit of fear, but of power and of love and of a sound mind." 2 Timothy 1:7.

"Peace I leave with you; my peace I give to you. I do not give to you as the world gives. Do not let your hearts be troubled and do not be afraid." John 14:27.

"Let us not become weary in doing good, for at the proper time we will reap a harvest if we do not give up." Galatians 6:9.

"Whenever I am afraid, I will trust in you." Psalm 56:3.

"You will keep in perfect peace him whose mind is steadfast, because he trusts in you." Isaiah 26:3.

Wait a minute.

Maybe I'd better back up. There is one verse which I consider to be the ultimate Survival Scripture because so many Christians base their faith on it. Even many Sunday school children could recite this one to you.

It is the beloved John 3:16: "For God so loved the world that he gave his only begotten son that whoever believeth in him should not perish but have eternal life."

God and Lucky Jack

Have you ever seen the movie, "Master and Commander: The Far Side of the World"?

The movie, starring Russell Crowe, is set during the Napoleonic Wars and tells the story of a British frigate captain called "Lucky Jack" Aubrey and his crew.

In the story, it is 1805 and Aubrey has orders to sink a French warship off the coast of South America. Aubrey will realize that the French ship has superior fire power and he must be extremely clever if he wants to defeat his enemy.

I first saw this movie with my husband, Chuck, and youngest son, Zach, in a theater a few years ago. I remember the almost dizzying battle scenes and the close relationship between the captain and the ship's more peace-loving surgeon.

But one scene struck me.

At this point, both ships are in the fog. Captain Jack sends out a decoy - a bunch of tied-together barrels with a sail and a lantern.

The trick works. The French ship takes off after the decoy.

Now I was just sure I knew what would happen next.

It was sheer genius.

I figured the British ship would follow the French warship and attack it from behind - probably its most vulnerable point.

Or so I thought.

Instead of following my brilliant plan, the British captain had his ship sneak away in the fog from its big foe.

Looking back, that made more sense, because ships in those days had cannons on the sides.

The British frigate would have had to turn at a 90-degree angle (so the two ships would have looked like a big, upside down "T" in the water) to fire at the back of the French ship.

Chuck says that would have been tough if the wind wasn't in the British ship's favor.

OK. I guess this means the U.S. Navy won't be calling me anytime soon to ask about my latest battle strategies.

But I think there are some lessons that can be learned from all of this.

For example, how many times do we go after that decoy - that distraction - and then take a hit at our most vulnerable point?

You know the common scenario: a man striving to get ahead at work follows the decoy called "Success Will Make Me Important, Wealthier and Happy." He takes on too many extra projects and loses touch with his family. Arguments follow. Then maybe even an extramarital affair.

And don't think for a moment that women can't fall into that trap, too.

Or how about this? We get so busy that we don't attend church, read our Bibles or pray. We go after the decoy of "Busyness" until we're shipwrecked on an island of trouble and despair.

Now, here this!

I'm not saying we shouldn't work hard. Or that we shouldn't do much-needed daily tasks. I'm not trying to torpedo anyone with a boatload of guilt.

Trust me. I know how busy life can get.

But I also know how important it is to make priorities.

And spending time with God, praying to him, reading his word and thinking about what it says are among those priorities.

As it says in 2 Peter 3:18: "But grow in the grace and knowledge of our Lord and Savior Jesus Christ."

It only makes sense. You can't drive a car without gas. Don't expect to run very well on an empty spiritual tank, either.

I can tell when my spiritual tank is running low. I'm not as tolerant or understanding - and I can get crabby fast.

So I find that I do best when I keep the tank topped off.

And I know that whether I'm going through smooth sailing or a stormy battle I want to be close to Christ, the master and commander of my ship, the captain of my soul.

An Extraordinary God

If you're like me, you wouldn't remember their names.

But you'd remember the situation.

In March 2005, Brian Nichols was accused of killing of four people, including a judge, in Atlanta, Ga.

But before he was caught, Nichols found his way to the apartment of a single mother named Ashley Smith.

Nichols held Smith hostage for seven hours. During that time, she read to him from the best-selling book, "The Purpose Driven Life," (Zondervan 2002) by Christian author Rick Warren.

In her own book, "Unlikely Angel," (Paigeturner, Inc. 2005) Smith also reportedly talks about her struggle with drugs and how she shared meth with Nichols.

But in news accounts, she said God gave her a choice that day: continue struggling with drugs or reach out to the Lord and be free of them.

Eventually, Nichols let Smith go. She called 911 and he surrendered.

Smith was hailed as a hero and said she gave up drugs.

Is she still off drugs today? I hope so. I hope she's turned her life around.

But what still amazes me about this story is how God let an ordinary person be thrust into extraordinary circumstances.

Then he allowed the miraculous to happen.

It reminds me of a man in the Bible named Gideon.

The story, found in the book of Judges, tells how the Israelites had fallen away from God, who let enemies, called the Midianites, destroy their crops and livestock - for years. Eventually the Israelites cried out to God.

And God sent an angel to Gideon.

"The Lord is with you, mighty warrior," the angel said.

But Gideon didn't see things that way. If the Lord was with them, then why were all these bad things happening?

Gideon decided that God had abandoned his people. Then Gideon rattled off a list of reasons why he'd be the last person to lead a battle.

But the angel wasn't dissuaded.

"Go in the strength you have," the angel said.

The angelic pep talk was probably encouraging, but Gideon still needed a lot of reassurance. So God performed some miracles for Gideon, helping build his confidence in his creator.

Then - greatly outnumbered - Gideon's forces prepared to meet the Midianites.

By this time, Gideon knew God would help him.

And Gideon had a plan.

He gave his men empty jars with torches inside of them and trumpets. They circled the enemy camp at night, blew the trumpets and smashed the jars. Holding the torches, they shouted "A sword for the Lord and for Gideon!"

Then the Bible says "While each man held his position around the camp, all the Midianites ran, crying out as they fled."

The Israelites then chased down and destroyed their enemies.

During Gideon's life, the Israelites enjoyed peace for 40 years.

Not bad for a guy who started out with a severe case of low self-esteem.

Today, I think people wonder why bad things have happened to them. Some believe God has forsaken them.

But God didn't abandon Gideon or Ashley Smith.

And I know in my heart he won't abandon us.

Sometimes, like Gideon, we need to step out in faith, in the strength we have, and watch God help our faith grow. Sometimes, like Gideon's men, we have to hold our position "around the camp," not always knowing what will happen, but trusting God.

Like Gideon, we may not feel like mighty warriors.

Maybe that's why it's good to remember people like Ashley Smith.

She wasn't a trained hostage negotiator or a counselor or a police officer.

But I believe God used her to prevent more killing and, in the process, showed her just how fragile life is.

She stepped out in the faith and strength she had. When she did, the extraordinary happened.

Which makes me think that we don't have to be extraordinary people.

We just have to believe in an extraordinary God.

Virginia's Calla Lily

One of the interesting things about working at the Tribune is that you never know who is going to walk in the door.

Or with what.

Years ago, we used to have wacky vegetable contests. People would bring a tomato or an eggplant with a cone-shaped protrusion that made it look as if the vegetable had a nose. It was kind of fun to watch the parade of bizarre garden produce.

But I never remember any unusual-looking flowers - and certainly nothing like the calla lily that Virginia Anderson brought the other day.

I've known Virginia for years. She was the one who started the citywide Thanksgiving dinner years ago so no one would have to spend the holiday alone. She's a nice Christian lady, who isn't afraid to share her faith.

When she came in, Virginia had some photographs and a story to tell.

Someone gave Virginia a calla lily for her 82nd birthday. She put it by the chair where she reads her Bible and prays. She'd had it three weeks, when one day she looked up and saw something different.

"I was pondering a situation that I was troubled about and I looked over at the lily and that's what I saw," she said, holding out the picture.

Now, in the center of a calla lily is a slim protrusion called a spadex. It is supposed to be shaped like a long, slender cigar, said Sarah Browning, an extension educator with the University of Nebraska-Lincoln.

But when Virginia looked at her lily, the spadex looked like a hand - giving a "thumbs up."

Virginia's troubled thoughts were replaced by a feeling of peace that flooded over her.

"It was like the Lord was saying, 'Everything is going to be all right," she said. "I had a presence of the Lord come over me."

Virginia added that the spadex hadn't looked like a hand until that day. What's more, the plant only had three flowers when she got it. Three weeks later, it had nine.

In the meantime, Virginia was so excited that she took the lily to Greens for Flowers in Fremont. There, designer Julie Hoffman took a look at it.

"I've been in the industry 27 years and I have yet to see anything like that," she told me on the telephone. "I've seen two iris out of one stem, but nothing like that. This is unusual."

I scanned one of Virginia's photos and e-mailed it to Sarah at the extension office.

Her reaction matched Julie's.

"To be honest, I've never seen one like this before," she said.

So is the center of Virginia's calla lily a fluke?

A simple abnormality of nature?

Or is it something more?

"I think God speaks to us through nature in so many facets and we just need to pay attention -- and (Virginia) did," Julie said.

Sarah expressed similar thoughts.

"I do think that God can send us signs in lots of different ways," Sarah said. "So this possibly could be an encouragement to her - that he's there watching over her."

You don't have to ask Virginia twice to see what she thinks.

"I knew it was a message from the Lord," she said.

Now, I've heard people snicker about a potato chip that supposedly looked like Star Trek's Capt. Kirk or other unusual things.

And they may do the same because of Virginia's calla lily.

But I hope they don't.

I know we live in a tough world, but have we become so cynical that we've stopped looking for touches of God in familiar places?

And is it so unusual to think that God would use a flower to comfort a believer with a troubled heart?

I don't think so.

Just look at the book of Matthew, chapter 6, starting with verse 25. Here Jesus says: "Therefore I tell you, do not worry about your life, what you will eat or drink; or about your body, what you will wear..."

Now, look at verse 28. Jesus says, "And why do you worry about clothes? See how the lilies of the field grow? They do not labor or spin. Yet I tell you that not even (King) Solomon in all his splendor was dressed like one of these."

Stop a minute. Did you notice that?

Jesus used lilies as an example.

Virginia's precious flower was a lily.

The very thought is enough to make me giddy.

Now from what I understand, Virginia's concerns weren't about food or clothing, but they are important. Yet even now, I know that Virginia has peace.

By the way, Julie gave Virginia some silica sand so she could preserve the lily. She also has photographs. But more than that, I think Virginia - and all of us - have a gentle reminder that God knows our concerns and remains ever ready to encourage those who seek him.

Even if it's through something as simple as a lily.

The Prayer of the Faithful

It happened week after week.

I could count on it.

Jerry Montayne came to the singles group that my husband, Chuck, and I led at our church on Wednesday nights.

Every Wednesday, I'd ask for prayer requests.

And every Wednesday, Jerry asked for one thing: that God would protect his cousin, Travis, and bring him home safely.

Travis Donnelly was a American soldier in Iraq. Then still in his early 20s, he was a cavalry scout - someone who gathers intelligence for the U.S. Army. His duties included searching for stored weapons, conducting raids and providing security at bases and checkpoints.

He had many close calls.

There was the time he was driving his Bradley tank down RPG alley, the nickname soldiers gave a street in tumultuous Fallujah. It was early one morning in May 2003.

By 2 a.m. it was getting hot.

And it was about to get hotter.

Unbeknownst to Travis and other soldiers in the tank, an RPG - a rocket-propelled grenade - was headed their way.

"There was a big explosion and it shifted the back of my Bradley when it hit," said Travis, then part of Fox Troop of the 3rd Armored Cavalry Regiment.

Travis, who typically drove with the hatch open about 12 inches, saw sparks flying from the right side of the tank. It startled him and he let up on the gas for a minute - then punched the accelerator. His tank commander spun the turret, fired on, and killed the man who'd launched the RPG.

Small arms fire continued.

Travis saw bullets fly off the tank, but got the vehicle to its intended destination - a dam they'd been ordered to guard. Soldiers assessed damage to the tank.

"A couple inches higher and it (the RPG) would have gone into the crew compartment where we have extra ammo and tows (missiles shot from the tank). It could have been really bad," he later said.

Another time Travis and other soldiers were on a roof, guarding a compound the in middle of Fallujah when some Iraqis scaled the side of the building and started throwing grenades.

It was his first firefight.

"The next thing I knew, there were explosions going on all around," he said.

His heart pounded as the roof shook and he was sprayed with small rocks from the explosions. Sounds of the blasts echoed in his ears.

It was a long night.

But Travis survived that night and many others.

Not everyone he knew was so fortunate.

His 29-year-old commander, Capt. Joshua T. Byers of Sparks, Nev., died when the Humvee he was in hit an explosive device during a convoy.

"He was an awesome Christian and a good man," Travis said.

The Associated Press recounted stories of Byers' heroics, including his reportedly tiptoeing in a minefield to rescue children who'd ventured there in search of firewood.

Various Web sites told how he left behind a wife, two brothers, and his parents who were Baptist missionaries in Guam. He died on his mother's birthday.

Travis continued his service in Iraq.

And Jerry - ever faithful - kept asking for prayer. Week after week. Sometimes Jerry gave us little reports about Travis.

Most of the time, our small group just prayed.

Then Travis came home.

Now out of the service, Travis and his wife, Melissa, have five children, Savannah, Siena and Gabriel. And on Dec. 12, 2008, Melissa gave birth to twins - a boy and a girl - Cash Montgomery and Cortina Julianna.

My heart warms whenever I've seen Travis and his lovely family in church. And when I see his cousin, Jerry, in the pew nearby, I can't help but smile.

The Bible says in James chapter 5 that the "prayer of a righteous man is powerful and effective." Travis has told me how he believes everyone's prayers helped and how grateful he is for Jerry's prayers.

Now, I don't know if I'll ever understand why Capt. Byers lost his life. But I'm so glad that Travis came home all right.

And I have to think that while Travis was on guard duty in Iraq, Jerry was on duty, too - back in the singles group as we turned to the only one who really could protect someone in danger so far away.

Thank you Lord for bringing Travis home.

And thank you Lord for Jerry, who remains an example of what it means to be faithful and consistent in prayer.

One Scrawny Calf

I heard a good story recently.

It came from Bill Michaud, a volunteer at the Low Income Ministry. At 81, Bill's been a volunteer at the Fremont center for about 13 years. Bill is the food pantry's buyer, purchasing everything from soup to cereal to keep the shelves stocked. But long before he volunteered there, Bill worked for the Iowa Breeders Association, selling supplies to farmers.

One time, back in the early 1970s, a dairy farmer wanted Bill and his boss to look at a Holstein bull calf in Canada for him. The two went to see the animal, then only about 3 or 4 months old.

"We were not overly impressed with it," Bill said. "It looked too scrawny."

The calf's legs even looked crooked.

Bill shared his thoughts with dairyman.

But that dairyman had a different perspective. The bull calf had a very good pedigree. So about six months later, he went to Canada, bought the bull for a fairly good price and brought it to the United States.

It never turned out to be a big bull - only about 1,400 to 1,500 pounds, compared to most which reach 1,600 to 1,800 pounds.

Yet that bull sired females who became top milk producers, something very valuable in the dairy world.

After a while, the farmer probably could have sold that bull for $10,000 to $15,000, which was a lot of money in those days, Bill said.

So what's the moral of the story?

You just can't judge a bull by its cover!

OK. All silliness aside, I think Bill's story shows how people judge by appearances. Now, Bill and his boss were supposed to evaluate that bull calf. And I'm not saying that you shouldn't avoid someone wearing a ski mask and running out of a bank. We live in a tough world and we have to be wise.

But I think people generally make a mistake when they judge each other by how they look instead of looking for something deeper.

One of the best examples can be found in the Bible. In 1 Samuel, chapter 16, we find a priest named Samuel who made a house call.

At that time, Israel wanted a king. God had Samuel anoint (pour oil on) a man named Saul, thus making him king. But Saul was a bad leader. So God picked someone else to be king and sent Samuel to anoint him. God had Samuel go to the home of a man named, Jesse, who had eight sons.

When he reached the man's house, Samuel saw one of the sons and figured that he surely must be the next king.

Not quite.

In verse 7, we read where Lord told Samuel: "Do not consider his appearance or his height, for I have rejected him. The Lord does not look at the things man looks at. Man looks at the outward appearance, but the Lord looks at the heart."

Seven of Jesse's sons passed in front of Samuel.

None of them would be the future king. Finally, Samuel asked if Jesse had any more sons.

"There's still the youngest," Jesse answered, "but he's tending the sheep."

Samuel wanted to see this boy, so they sent for him.

The son came in.

"Rise and anoint him; he is the one," the Lord told Samuel.

So Samuel anointed a young man named David.

Name sound familiar? This David went on to kill a giant named Goliath. And while the road to the throne was long and difficult, David eventually became king of Israel. He made many mistakes and had many sorrows, yet he would be called a man after God's own heart.

Wanna a glimpse into David's heart?

Just look into the Psalms. He wrote many of them. Remember

the beloved 23rd Psalm? It starts out like this: "The Lord is my shepherd; I shall not be in want. He makes me to lie down in green pastures, he leads me besides quiet waters, he restores my soul...."

Who could write that better than someone - like David - who was a shepherd?

Feeling a little scared about something? David understood fear. Yet look what he wrote in Psalm 34:4: "I sought the Lord and he answered me; he delivered me from all my fears."

David knew his source of strength. And God knew David. So even if nobody else could picture David as a future king, God knew the young man's potential, his heart and his destiny.

And just like that dairyman saw something different in that scrawny bull calf, God saw something different in David. Something he could use and mold and guide.

Now I'm sure nobody would ask me to judge a calf, but I pray that God helps me see people with his eyes. And I hope that I can look at people - not only for what they seem like now - but for what they can become.

I think that's how God sees us.

Not as a scrawny calf.

Or some little shepherd kid.

But as someone with priceless potential.

A Writer's Testimony

As I sat across the table from her, my lunch pal had an interesting question.

"How did you get the passion ... get to the place where you are now?"

We were talking about my Christian faith and the question took me back to the beginning.

Well, almost.

I'd gone to church all my life. I was baptized as an infant and later confirmed in the Lutheran Church Missouri Synod. My mom taught Sunday school. I remember going to some Sunday School classes and to vacation Bible school.

But it wasn't until I was 16 years old that I really found out what Christianity was really all about.

Now, my mom had wanted me to be in the church youth group and before I knew it I was sitting with some kids from church. Back then, they voted you into the group. So as a kid who'd been picked on most of her school years, it felt good to be selected unanimously for something.

I hope I never forget seeing their raised hands and smiling faces.

Then late one afternoon we were gathered for a special activity at the church.

I was sitting on a piano bench in the church basement when the man came up to me. I can't remember his name or even his face, but I will be eternally grateful for the question he asked me.

Now - prepare yourself - the question he asked may seem pretty blunt to some, but it became a turning point in my life.

"If you were to die tonight, how do you know if you'd go to heaven?" he asked.

I paused for a moment.

I was teenager and death seemed like something that would only happen in the very distant future.

I'd never thought about that before. I didn't know for sure.

Then he told me that everyone is a sinner. None of us is perfect. But if we repent of our sins and believe that Jesus died on the cross to save us from our sins (and rose again) then we can be assured we can go to heaven.

Please let me stop and explain repentance, because I didn't totally know what it meant or entailed at first.

To repent means to be so sorry for our sins that we never want to do them again. It doesn't mean we're going to be perfect or never make mistakes. When we do, we ask forgiveness. And it doesn't mean that we say "Oh I'll do this tonight and say I'm sorry tomorrow."

We just try to live each day doing what Jesus would want us to do.

It's not easy, but it's worth it.

Anyway, even as a teen, I decided that I wanted that assurance. The man prayed with me and I asked Jesus to come into my heart and be my savior.

I think I went on a three-day spiritual "high" after that. I was happy. I felt as if I had reached some new spiritual height with God.

The man who came to our church was there to launch a program called "Ongoing Ambassadors for Christ." Teens from several churches met once each month in a different town. We'd have music and prayer on Friday evening, stay at a host's home and then the next day we'd go door to door - basically asking the same question the man asked me, but as part of a survey.

It was fun.

People didn't seem to mind hearing what we had to share.

I stayed active with that group for quite a while, but then it seemed like the world started pulling me away.

Monday morning when I'd come back from the weekend, I'd listen to my school friends talk about their Saturday night parties and the fun they had.

I started feeling like I was missing out. Once the girl who couldn't wait to share the Gospel, I started talking about it less.

Gradually, I slipped away, hanging out more with my school friends, partying, doing things I shouldn't.

I graduated from high school and went to college. I don't think I went to church more than six times during those four years. I graduated and started working.

I was lonely, but God put a wonderful Christian woman in my life. I began attending Bible study and an Assemblies of God church with her.

Then my lifestyle caught up with me.

I got pregnant and wasn't married. I became a single parent.

If ever I needed God, it was now.

The years that followed were extremely difficult, but God gave me a nonjudgmental church family who just loved me.

If I am passionate about Christ, it is because I know what he's done for me - how he's reached into the darkest times of my life and brought me hope and strength. Am I perfect? Absolutely not. I mess up, make mistakes, say things I shouldn't.

But I know without a doubt that Jesus died for me and someday I will be in heaven with him.

I know it.

A Fish Story

I seriously doubt you'll ever see me on the cover of a fishing magazine.

My lack of skill could have something to do with that.

Years ago, my high school boyfriend and his family took me fishing on their boat. I quickly discovered that I was terrible at this sport.

Why?

Perhaps it's because I lost one of their favorite fishing poles while we were trolling. I was assigned to watch it. I thought it was hooked securely to the boat.

Or maybe I was supposed to hold it.

I can't remember.

But I do remember the next fishing fiasco, which occurred while I was holding a fish by the line. My boyfriend was sitting in the boat.

Honestly, I didn't mean to drop the fish on his leg. And I had no idea that their fins were so sharp. If I hadn't seen it with my own eyes, I never would have believed that the fin could slice a hairline-thin cut into someone's flesh.

Amazingly, both my boyfriend and his dad took everything in stride. They didn't dump me overboard. Then again, they knew I couldn't swim. Maybe they didn't want to feel obligated to save me.

All such tales aside, I am reminded of several fish stories from the Bible. One occurs in the New Testament book of Luke, chapter 5.

It involves Peter, who is a fisherman. On this particular day, Christ is preaching by the Lake of Gennesaret when he gets into Peter's boat and asks him to put out a little way from shore. Then Jesus sits and teaches people from the boat.

When he finishes, Christ tells Peter to go out into the deep water and let down the nets for a catch.

I can just imagine the astonished look on Peter's face.

"Master, we've worked hard all night and haven't caught anything. But because you say so, I will let down the nets," Peter says.

When Peter and those with him follow Christ's direction, they catch so many fish their nets start to break. Fishing partners in another boat come to help and they fill both boats so full that they begin to sink.

Then Peter falls to his knees and says "Go away from me Lord; I am a sinful man."

Now, why would Peter tell Jesus - who just supplied such an amazing blessing - to leave?

Could it be that when Peter encounters such holy greatness that he is made painfully - even fearfully - aware of his own faults?

But gentle Jesus tells Peter not to be afraid.

"From now on you will catch men," Jesus says, after which Peter and two partners, James and John, leave everything and follow Christ.

Sounds like a great beginning, right?

But oh my, Peter will face his own shortcomings and learn some difficult lessons as he walks with his Lord.

One tough lesson occurs after Peter emotionally announces that he will die with Christ - only to deny even knowing him on three separate occasions.

Then comes a scene that I find so beautiful and poignant. It shows a situation that has come full circle.

To me, it's like the end of a movie which draws back to a wonderful, familiar scene that we saw when the film began.

Found in the book of John, chapter 21, it takes place after Christ's crucifixion and resurrection. At this point, Christ has already appeared twice to his disciples.

One night, Peter decides to go back to one of the things he knows best - fishing. Others follow, but the group doesn't catch anything.

The next morning, Jesus is standing on the shore, yet his own disciples don't recognize him.

"Friends, haven't you any fish?" Jesus calls out.

"No," they answer.

"Throw your net on the right side of the boat and you will find some," Jesus says.

When they do, they find the net so full of fish that they can't haul it into the boat.

Gee, where have we seen this scene before? Doesn't it seem like deja vu?

Imagine the men fumbling with all those fish, when a disciple notices Jesus and excitedly tells Peter, "It is the Lord!"

Peter wastes no time. He jumps in the water and swims to Christ, leaving the other disciples to follow in the boat with the net in tow.

They land and see a fire of burning coals with fish on it and bread.

Jesus tells the disciples to bring some of the fish they caught. Peter drags the net ashore.

It has to be a fisherman's dream: 153 large fish.

Jesus then asks the men to eat what he prepared.

When I read this story I see the love, forgiveness and mercy of Jesus. Why should Jesus have done anything for these guys? All the disciples ran away when soldiers came to take Christ to his death. And Peter later denied knowing him.

But here we see Jesus on the shore providing another incredible miracle and then cooking their breakfast.

I see Christ showing his disciples that God can supply all their needs.

And I see Jesus letting Peter know that he's got a second chance to start catching, not fish but men.

Toward the end of the chapter, Jesus asks three times if Peter loves him. Each time Peter says "yes." I wonder if Jesus was asking, not for himself, but so Peter could reconcile it in his own heart and mind. Then Christ asks Peter to "feed my sheep." Here, I believe Christ was telling Peter to begin serving up hefty portions - not of fish - but of the Gospel and God's love.

And maybe Christ was saying that even when we mess up, he can still take us back to the place where we started - then give us a fresh start.

I'm sure glad for all the second chances that God has given me - even if none of them involved fishing.

And I'd like to think that somewhere my old high school boyfriend would smile if he heard that the closest I get to fishing these days is when I open a can of tuna.

The Reward of Loyalty

Last summer, I saw a story I had to save.

The headline read: "Dog guarded owner's body after death." The Associated Press story told how a German shepherd stood guard over the body of a Colorado man for six weeks. The 25-year-old man, whose death was ruled a suicide, was found in the remote northeastern Colorado plains.

The man's dog named, Cash, was found beside him. She was thin and dehydrated, but alive. Authorities suspected she survived by eating mice and rabbits. Investigators believed the dog kept coyotes away from the man's body.

Cash was reunited with the man's wife and toddler son. I'm sure the man's death was a blow to his family, but I suspect they were touched by the dog's loyalty.

The story makes me sad. I wonder what drove the man to such hopelessness. And I can just imagine the confused animal trying to figure out what happened, then resolutely guarding the master who'd once cared for her.

Now I've known of people who sat by the hospital beds of their loved ones for years, stayed in difficult marriages, tended to aging family members. But like others, I've seen harsh betrayals, both short and long term.

We wonder why those things happen. Yet the Bible is filled with stories of betrayal. Perhaps the saddest takes place right before Jesus dies on the cross. The story begins in the New Testament book of Matthew starting with chapter 26.

The religious leaders of that day wanted to kill Jesus. Later, in verse 14, we see one of Christ's disciples, a man named Judas Iscariot, paying them a visit. He wants to know what they'll give him if he hands Jesus over to them.

I wonder how Judas heard about their plot. I guess word gets around.

And if you look in the book of John, chapter 12, you get a glimpse into the nature of Judas as he objects when expensive perfume is poured on Christ's feet. Judas complains that the perfume could have been sold and the money given to the poor.

But look what the text says next about Judas: "He didn't say this because he cared about the poor, but because he was a thief; as keeper of the money bag, he used to help himself to what was put into it."

The man was an ancient-day embezzler.

Back in the book of Matthew, we see that the religious leaders give Judas 30 silver coins after which he seeks a way to betray Jesus.

It's hard to imagine that someone would be so greedy that he would conspire against the man - the son of God - who healed the sick, fed the multitudes and blessed children. I guess the shine of those silver coins must have helped blind Judas to such things.

At the last supper Jesus ever has with his disciples, he even identifies Judas as the one who will betray him.

"Surely not I," Judas says.

Doesn't seem like Judas is above lying, either.

In other accounts, Jesus then tells Judas to do what he needs to do and the traitor heads out. Later we see Jesus praying in a place called Gethsemane. His disciples are with him when Judas shows up with a large crowd armed with swords and clubs, sent by those scheming religious leaders.

Judas even has a secret code of sorts and tells the henchmen with him: "The one I kiss is the man; arrest him."

Then he greets Jesus and gives him a kiss.

Now, if I was getting that kiss of betrayal, I'd want to slug Judas. But listen to Jesus, who says "Friend, do what you came for."

Friend? Judas?

Somehow those two words don't fit together - at least not in my understanding.

Then I have to think how Christ probably saw it. He knew he had to die to save us. He knew he was - and still is - the bridge between a fallen people and a holy God.

So he calls the man - that wayward child of God - a friend.

Christ is taken away and crucified. In chapter 27, it says that Judas, "seized with remorse," returns the silver coins and kills himself.

And what about Christ's other disciples?

They don't exactly get gold stars, either. They run off when the crowd comes to haul Jesus away. Peter later denies even knowing Jesus.

Good grief. Maybe it would have been nicer for Jesus if he'd forgotten all about human friends.

Maybe he should have just gotten a dog.

But I'm so glad he didn't give up on us. He died on the cross to save us from our sins. (And no human is perfect.) Now, if we repent of our sins, believe Christ died on the cross to save us and ask him to come into our hearts and be our savior, we'll go to heaven some day.

Those familiar with the rest of the story know Jesus rose from the grave and even visited those runaway disciples - almost all of whom would later give their lives spreading the Gospel.

In the end, all but Judas turned out to be loyal to the one who gave his life for them.

That's the kind of loyalty I want.

The kind I pray for.

In the end of the modern-day story, Cash the dog was rewarded for her loyalty.

She got to go home. She got to see those who loved her and were waiting for her.

And in God's timing - not mine - that's what I want some day, too.

To go home to heaven and see those who love me and are waiting for me.

Nobody's Perfect

"Nobody's perfect."

"I'm only human."

"Everybody makes mistakes."

How many times have you heard those sayings?

Many of us believe them.

So why do we think we have to be perfect to come to God? How many of us think that we'll start reading our Bible or going to church or seeking God after we get our lives straightened up a little bit?

Can I tell you something?

Don't wait.

God loves you right where you are.

My husband, Chuck, says it like this: "Waiting until you're perfect to come to God is like trying to get all cleaned up before you take your bath."

What's the point? And who gets us cleaned up better than God and helps us to become the people we never even dreamed we could become?

I'm sure glad a woman named Rahab didn't think she had to be perfect to trust God.

Her story is found in the Old Testament book of Joshua, starting in the second chapter.

At this point, God's chosen people - the Israelites - plan to enter the land that the Lord promised to give them. But they'll have to conquer the formidable city of Jericho first.

So, their leader, Joshua, sends in a couple of spies.

What are their names? I dunno. They were spies.

Anyway, they stay at Rahab's house.

Now Rahab isn't your ordinary hostess. She's a prostitute. But she knows enough about the Lord to realize that he's the only one true God. So she hides the spies and even lies about it to Jericho's king. Now, I don't condone lying at all, but Rahab probably had some issues to work through.

At any rate, she helps the spies escape. But before they leave, she asks them to save her family. They agree. They tell her to gather her family in her home and tie a scarlet cord in the window so the Israelites will know whom to spare when they take the city. They warn her that they can't be responsible if someone leaves her home and is killed.

The spies escape and tell Joshua everything.

Then God gives Joshua some marching orders.

The armed men of Israel are to march around the city - which is surrounded by a big wall - once each day for six days. On the seventh day, they march around seven times. When priests who are with them sound a long blast on their trumpets, the Israelites are to shout, then the city's wall will collapse.

Did I mention that Rahab's house is part of the city wall?

Well, as planned, the Israelites march around the city and take it after the wall collapses on the seventh day.

I try to imagine Rahab gathering her family together and keeping them in that house. They must have been terrified when they saw the Israelites marching around Jericho day after day. I don't think the spies sent Rahab an e-mail to let her know the plan.

And on that seventh day, how did she keep her wits and her family together in that house when everything around her literally was falling apart?

Talk about hanging by a thread.

Everything seemed to depend on that red cord in the window. Rahab had to have incredible faith that God would protect her and that those spies would keep their word.

And God was faithful.

Joshua sent the spies to bring Rahab and her family to safety.

And guess what?

If you look in the first chapter of Matthew, in the New Testament, you can read the geneaology of Jesus. Guess who was one of Jesus' ancestors?

Yep. It was Rahab.

From what I've read, she married an Israelite named Salmon

and had a son named Boaz. And so the line continued. Looks like God didn't mind having somebody like Rahab in Jesus' family tree.

Rahab also gets a nice mention in the New Testament book of Hebrews.

In this text, the writer is talking about the great people of faith. He tells about Abraham, Jacob and Moses. Then in verse 11, he writes: "By faith the prostitute Rahab, because she welcomed the spies, was not killed with those who were disobedient."

Imagine that. The writer could have talked about Deborah, a judge in Israel. Or Mary, the mother of Jesus. Or Elizabeth, the mother of John the Baptist.

But nope. He wrote about Rahab.

She wasn't perfect.

Oh, but I love what Christian author Beth Moore writes about Rahab in the workbook, "Believing God"*: "(Rahab's) exercise of faith did not come after Rahab went to rehab ... She believed God first and then let him clean up her act."

Rahab's story is one of redemption - which is what Jesus is all about.

Christ died an agonizing death on a cross so those who repent of their sins, believe in him and ask him to come into their hearts can live in heaven forever.

And he doesn't play favorites.

When Jesus was dying on that cross, I don't think he told himself, "OK, I'm basically doing this for everybody - but I'm really doing this for my disciple, Peter, and my mother and for that guy named Billy Graham. He's really going to be something someday."

No. I don't believe for a moment that Jesus loves Moses or Peter or even Rahab more than anybody else.

I believe while he was dying on the cross, Jesus thought of the billions of imperfect, flawed people - like you and me - and decided that he'd rather die than to live without us forever.

For that I will be eternally grateful.

*Used by permission of Lifeway Christian Resources.

An Angel Named Henry

His name was Henry.

I met him in the cafeteria at Omaha's Clarkson Hospital.

It was 1996 and my dad was on dialysis. He'd been so sick and gotten so thin and we'd made so many trips to Omaha that I was sad and tired and worn out.

Dad always wanted me to eat supper while he was having a treatment so I'd become well-acquainted with the hospital's big-windowed cafeteria.

I'd also become used to eating by myself, often taking a book along to read. But that particular day, I noticed a small man at the next table. He was wiry and looked like he'd worked hard all of his life.

He also was very friendly and we started up a conversation. Before I knew it, I'd carried my tray to his table and we were chatting like old friends.

Henry said his wife had been sick and in the hospital. He also said he'd done some demolition work for a Fremont company that was expanding its business.

For a moment, I felt a touch of home. And somehow - for that brief time - I forgot about my heartache.

Now Henry was probably an ordinary guy. But sometimes even today I wonder if he was an angel.

At any rate, he was an angel to me.

Or maybe he was just a Good Samaritan with a lunch tray.

Most people know the familiar Bible story. A man is robbed, beaten and left for dead along a roadside.

A couple of church-operating folks - a priest and a Levite - pass by without helping.

Then a Samaritan - one of a group of greatly disliked people - stops to help the man, tending to his wounds and taking him to an inn. The Samaritan even pays for the guy to stay there and says he'll pay any extra fees necessary when he passes through again.

Now you don't have to be physically beaten to feel as if life has pummeled you to a pulp. That's when we need a Good Samaritan to help "bandage" the wounds - even if it's with a kind word, a Scripture or a prayer.

But I can also identify all too well with the guys who passed by the hurting man.

They might have been frightened that robbers still lurked nearby.

Maybe they also bore the weight of numerous responsibilities. Did they worry about getting everything done? Were they already late and concerned people would be mad? Or were they just tired?

I know how I've struggled with trying to juggle time, responsibility and weariness while knowing people who could use a couple of hours of conversation.

And what does Proverbs 12:25 say? "An anxious heart weighs a man down, but a kind word cheers him up."

Oh boy. Sounds like I'd better get busy. But before I head into guilt overload, let me say that we can all ask God to provide us pockets of time and help us manage it. We can trust him to give us increased energy and show us how to be Better Samaritans.

Then we can dump that guilt by the side of the road.

I've never seen Henry since that day in the cafeteria. I wonder if I'd even recognize him now.

Time can fog the memory.

But one thing I will remember: That for a brief time, a small, friendly man made life a little easier for me.

Our Shield and Very Great Reward

I love to hear Cherrie Beam Clarke tell stories.

As a storyteller with the Nebraska Humanities Council, she creates a character named Mariah Monahan who tells listeners what life was like for early settlers.

Cherrie's descriptions are so vivid that I can almost see the 12-foot-high flames of a prairie fire.

Or swarms of grasshoppers eating garments right off a clothes-line.

Or a family trying to cross a river in a covered wagon loaded with children.

Tears come to my eyes when I think of the sacrifices that early pioneers made to settle this land we now call Nebraska. They left friends and family and everything they knew behind to try to make a better life for themselves.

They also remind me of a man named Abraham from the Bible. Centuries before settlers ever loaded wagons and headed west across the vast plains of the United States, God told a man named Abram (later renamed Abraham) to leave his country, his people and his father's household and "go to the land I show you."

Why would God do that?

In Genesis chapter 12, we learn that God promised to make Abraham's descendants into a great nation.

Those descendants would later be called Israelites and eventually Jews - God's chosen people and the ones from whom Jesus would come.

But before any of that could happen, Abraham had to set out for new territory.

You almost wonder why Abraham couldn't build a great nation in his own hometown. But in her wonderful workbook/DVD study called "The Patriarchs," Christian author Beth Moore explains.*

Abraham, she said, lived in the city of Ur in Mesopotamia in the Middle East. The people there, including Abraham's own father, worshipped many gods.

One of those gods was Nanna, the moon god and the city patron. And to earn his favor, "worshippers served him with endless offerings, sacrifices and demeaning rituals," Moore writes.

Doesn't sound like much fun.

But Abraham didn't seem to follow the crowd.

"Bits of Hebrew tradition teach that Abram refused to participate in his family's religious practices, implying that God called him because he was set apart from the others from the start," Moore writes.

I'd like to think that Abraham really was different and that God saw something in this man that he could mold and use and direct. First, however, God needed to get him away from some bad, old influences. So with scant instructions, God told Abraham to head out to a new land.

And Abraham did.

He packed up his wife and belongings - and at age 75 - became what we might call a Middle Eastern pioneer.

It couldn't have been easy - leaving everything behind. Not knowing where he was going. Just trusting God who told him to go.

However God also gave Abraham a wonderful promise. In Genesis 15:1 we read where God said: "Do not be afraid, Abram. I am your shield, your very great reward."

Whenever I read this verse, I take it personally. I believe God is telling me not to be afraid - no matter what circumstances I face - because he is my shield and my very great reward.

And I have found that to be true after a long day at work or when facing what could be a tense situation with someone or when I'm just tired.

He is the God who brings me hope and joy.

I imagine God did the same for Abraham and for many of our early Nebraska pioneers.

You know, I've always heard that pioneers were self-sufficient. But I think to survive and thrive pioneers probably had to be more God-dependent than self-reliant.

What else could they do when grasshoppers ate their crops down to nothing or when a prairie fire threatened their home or as they sat by the bed of a very sick child in a blizzard? What could they do as they sat in a covered wagon and saw a tornado headed their way? How many settlers prayed, clung to their faith and trusted in God to get them through life's difficult circumstances?

When I think of all the conveniences I have today - a washer and dryer, a dishwasher, a hospital only blocks away and a microwave oven for my food - I'm so grateful for settlers who were willing to go to a land they did not know.

And as I read through the Bible, I'm thankful for a man named Abraham who followed God's call, paved the way for a nation and became the ancestor of our Lord and Savior Jesus Christ.

*Used by permission of Lifeway Christian Resources

The Godly Aunt

Her name was Jehosheba.

Not a well-known name as far as Bible stories go.

But she did something that I think was very brave and compassionate.

Her story is found in the Old Testament books of 2 Kings and 2 Chronicles.

In these accounts, an evil queen named, Athaliah, is so determined to stay in power that she's destroying an entire royal family, which includes a little prince named Joash.

That's where his aunt - a woman named Jehosheba - steps in. She steals the baby away and hides him and his nurse in the temple.

Joash remains safely in the temple for six years. When he turns 7, his uncle who is a priest - and Jehosheba's husband - finds men to guard the child, then crowns him king. The people are happy, but mean queen Athaliah is not.

"Treason, treason!" she shouts.

To make a long story short, she is put to death and Joash is kept safe.

Now, I wish I could say this story had a happy ending.

But not all Bible stories do.

Little King Joash grows up and while under his uncle's mentoring seems to do pretty well.

Then after his uncle dies, Joash starts listening to the wrong people.

He forgets about God. And when the Lord sends Godly people to talk to Joash, he won't listen.

Worse yet, he has his own cousin (his late uncle's son) murdered.

In the end, King Joash is killed, too.

OK. This is not a heart-warming story.

So why am I sharing it?

Maybe it's because I'm so touched by the actions of Joash's aunt. Remember her? Her name is Jehosheba. She is the woman who probably risked her own life to save little Joash and carry him away to safety in God's house.

She didn't have to do that. She could have just gone to the temple by herself and hid out with her husband.

Instead, she got involved.

Her story makes me think about my own nieces and nephews - and my role as an aunt.

I don't have to whisk them away from an evil queen, but do I bring them to God's house where they can learn about the Lord and worship him? Do I teach them how important it is to trust God - how much he loves them and how he can help them through the darkest times in their lives? Do I tell them how vital it is to talk to him - not with formal, stilted words, but from the heart?

My own extended family has been spread out across the country, but I remember times spent with aunts, uncles and cousins when I was a child. We may not have had long or frequent times, but many of them made definite impressions on me.

As a child, I remember how nice it was to have the love and affirmation of adults - other than my parents and grandparents. I still smile at my Uncle Frank's goofy pranks, the gentleness of my uncles Bud and Rick and my Aunt Ena's wisdom. I remember how much fun I had with that Creepy Crawlers set my Uncle Don got me one year for Christmas. I think of Aunt Dorothy every time I wear "White Shoulders" perfume.

A couple of my relatives are gone now, but I still see their faces - snapshots of a distance past - in my mind's eye.

Now I guess that I'm the generation up to bat. How will my nieces and nephews remember me? My prayer is that they remember me as a woman of faith, who loved them and tried to point them toward their Lord.

In talking with my husband, Chuck, about this Bible story, he noticed something else. King Joash started messing up after the death of his uncle, who'd been his mentor. Chuck said he believes that's why it's important that we all keep good mentors around us - those people who provide Godly counsel and guidance. And I think it's also important that we be good mentors to those who will follow after us.

If I'm any sort of a good aunt at all these days, it's because of the wonderful role models I had as a child. I took it for granted then, but now I'm starting to realize just how much God blessed me with aunts and uncles who loved me as I was, saw my potential and wanted the best for me.

I can only hope to do so well.

The Water at Marah

Are you still upset about a terrible Christmas gift you got?

A few weeks ago, the Fremont Tribune asked readers to tell us about their worst Christmas gifts.

I was amazed at responses I read in an article by Copy Editor Leeanna Ellis. I cringed at these gifts-turned-insults - everything from a used sweater with a cigarette burn to baskets of meat and cheese that had expired by at least seven years. I got the feeling that the gift-givers had the money to buy something better, but chose not to.

Such stories remind me of one my dad told years ago. He never forgot the Christmas when relatives gave him a pair of wire-cutters as a gift. I guess they thought he could use those to fix his fences on the farm.

But his fences didn't need fixing. And fence repair wasn't exactly his favorite pastime.

He wasn't pleased.

To make matters worse, other relatives seemed to get nice, personal gifts.

It was one of many slights for my dad. And as time passed, the offenses and insults piled up like grain in a bin.

What happens when offenses pile up?

I think they can turn into bitterness.

Christian author Beth Moore talks about bitterness in her DVD/ workbook study called "A Woman's Heart: God's Dwelling Place."*

She takes readers to a little-noticed Bible story in Exodus 15:22-27.

By the time this account takes place, these things have already happened:

* God has sent 10 plagues on the Egyptians who enslaved the Israelites.

* Moses has led the Israelites out of Egypt.

* They've watched as God parted the Red Sea. They've crossed in safety, but the water has drowned the Egyptian army that sought to recapture them.

They've already seen plenty of miracles.

Then they reach the Desert of Shur.

They travel three days without finding water. Finally, they reach a place called Marah, but they can't drink the water here because it's bitter.

Needless to say, they're not happy campers.

They grumble and their leader, Moses, cries out to God.

God then shows Moses a piece of wood (the King James Version of the Bible calls it a tree).

Either way, Moses throws the wood into the water, which becomes sweet.

The Lord then basically tells the Israelites that if they listen to him - and do what he says - that he won't bring any of the diseases on them that he brought on the Egyptians.

What does bitter water have to do with disease?

Moore says God was "demonstrating his power over the most common disease from which his children would suffer - bitterness."

She says "Bitterness is spiritual cancer, a rapidly-growing malignancy that can consume your life."

I've also heard bitterness and unforgiveness described as an acid that eats the vessel which holds it.

I've heard it described as poison.

Christian author and speaker Joyce Meyer says harboring unforgiveness is like drinking poison, hoping that it kills your enemy. She tells about a time that someone hurt her.

She chose to forgive, wouldn't talk bad about them, prayed every day for God to bless them - and asked God to restore what could be restored.

It didn't mean her feelings weren't hurt, but I believe God brought her healing. Eventually, that relationship was restored.

I would add that we also need to ask God to heal us and to help us forgive. By forgiving, we drain that acid, that poison, that bitterness out of our hearts - thus doing ourselves a great service.

As I think about the Israelites and the water at Marah, I wonder if they learned that only God can heal bitterness and bring sweetness in its place.

And to anyone who's ever gotten a lousy gift - or no gift at all - let me tell you how sorry I am that this happened to you.

I pray that God has - or will - heal your heart and that you can know freedom from bitterness and unforgiveness.

More than anything, I hope you will come to know God's greatest gift to us - his only son, Jesus Christ.

*Used by permission of Lifeway Christian Resources

The Automatic Lesson

I don't want much.

I just want self-cleaning windows and floors.

How about windows with decorative, enclosed boxes underneath?

You'd press a button and cleaning fluid would squirt onto the windows. Then huge wipers would clean away the fluid and grime and then go right back into that box.

Think of the paper towels you'd save!

Or how about a remote-controlled, specially shaped (not round) mechanical device that could clean around and behind toilets?

Or what about an automatic sandwich maker?

It would be self-contained in an attractive countertop box with a viewing window. A piece of bread would drop. Then peanut butter would squirt from one side of the device and jelly from the other. Then the other piece of bread would drop. You could have refrigerated jelly in a tube to squeeze into the machine. You could dump crumbs from a removable tray at the bottom of the device.

OK. Maybe I'm letting my imagination run too wild. Maybe I've watched too many science fiction shows. Or perhaps too many episodes of "Wallace and Gromit." Have you seen this British program? A wacky inventor, named Wallace, pushes a button so his bed upends, sending him down through an opening in the floor and into a chair for breakfast - right next to his newspaper-reading dog.

If only life could be so easy.

But for some things, I guess there are no shortcuts.

Take prayer and Bible study, for instance.

It's true that there are lots of wonderful aids like recordings of the entire Bible. Or innumerable CDs featuring Bible teachers and speakers. Turn on the television and you might see a broadcast of a local church service or a service hundreds of miles away.

Yet nothing takes the place of sitting down, kneeling or taking a walk and talking to God. And nothing can replace reading the Bible or doing a study where you must look up Scripture.

Even the Bible talks about the importance of ... well ... reading the Bible.

The writer of Psalms 119:105 writes: "Your word is a lamp to my feet and a light to my path."

Then there's Psalms 119:130: "The unfolding of your word gives light, it gives understanding to the simple."

I don't know how many times I've sat down to the Bible with a problem and gained an answer or insight or a very good reminder of what I should do or how I should act.

And as I've meditated on God's word (thought about it repeatedly), it's become part of me - likely to pop up in my brain just when I need it.

I truly believe the Bible isn't just some boring, old book.

God speaks through his word.

As the writer of Hebrews 4:12 says: "For the word of God is living and active. Sharper than any double-edged sword, it penetrates even to dividing soul and spirit, joints and marrow; it judges the thoughts and attitudes of the heart."

Don't let that scare you.

I believe it's true that reading God's word can expose an ugly, hidden motive like a mirror can expose a pimple. If that's the case, I think we need to repent and ask God to help us do better. But I believe God's word can also be wonderfully encouraging and confirm good attitudes and behaviors.

Ever read: "A merry heart doeth good like a medicine....?"

I often think of that verse when I'm in a good mood.

Then there's one of my all-time favorite Psalms; it's the very first chapter of that book.

It reads:

"Blessed is the man who does not walk in the counsel of the wicked or stand in the way of sinners or sit in the seat of mockers. But his delight is in the law of the Lord and on his law, he meditates day and night.

He is like a tree, planted by streams of water, which yields its fruit in season and whose leaf does not wither. Whatever he does prospers."

To me, that verse says to seek Godly counsel and avoid those who want to do wrong, gossip and make fun of others. But I think it also shows how beneficial it is to keep God's word in mind.

Speaking of beneficial, I might to well to rethink some of my invention ideas. I can already see some things that could go wrong.

For instance, what if the fluid in the window boxes freezes? I guess the homeowner would have to be sure and drain them each fall.

Oh, and what if my mechanical floor cleaner gets stuck behind the toilet? It would have to be a pretty narrow device.

Oops. And what if the peanut butter gets dry and crusty and won't squirt out on the bread? Somebody will have to be sure and keep that machine clean.

I'm guessing an inventor would have to work out a few possible flaws in my dream inventions.

But there's one great thing about the word of God.

As Proverbs 30:5 says "Every word of God is flawless; he is a shield to those who take refuge in him."

The God of Second Chances

Leo got a second chance.

For all practical purposes, Leo was on death row when he and other pit bulls were rescued from Michael Vick's dogfighting stables last year. Vick, a former NFL quarterback now serving prison time, had bankrolled the dogfighting operation. News reports said when officers raided his Bad Newz Kennels in Smithville, Va., they found injured and scarred dogs. They also found the remains of dogs that had been shot, electrocuted, drowned, hanged or slammed to the ground for not wanting to fight.

And they found Leo confined in heavy chains.

I learned about Leo on MSNBC.com* and started reading the story to my husband, Chuck. I almost couldn't get through it. Officials, the story said, rescued 50 dogs, but there's always a concern whether fighting dogs can be trusted.

A trainer named Marthina McClay took a chance on Leo. Today, Leo lives in California, visiting patients undergoing chemotherapy at a cancer center and young men on probation at another center.

Cancer patients love the dog they see as a survivor. The young men consider the once-tough dog's terrible background and learn that they can become whatever they want to be.

Leo is one example of a life redeemed - in his case literally - from the pit, but the Bible is filled with stories about people who got a second chance.

Jonah

Remember Jonah? He ran the other way when God told him to warn the people of Ninevah to change their evil lifestyles or face destruction. The disobedient prophet boarded a boat, got tossed overboard in a bad storm and became the catch of the day for some big fish.

I guess Jonah needed time to think things over in that fish's belly. Anyway, Jonah repented and after three days was vomited up on a beach.

Not a pretty picture.

The point is: Jonah got a second chance.

Then he did what he was told - and thousands of people were saved.

Zacchaeus

What about Zacchaeus? He was a short man, physically, but not short on faith. This little tax collector even climbed a tree to see Jesus. Now tax collectors were despised in Jesus' day because they cheated people and the crowd didn't like it when Jesus wanted to be this guy's dinner guest.

But in Luke chapter 19 we see that Zacchaeus was ready to make a change in his life.

"Look Lord, here and now I give half my possessions to the poor, and if I have cheated anybody out of anything, I will pay back four times the amount," Zacchaeus said.

Zacchaeus just wanted a second chance - something Jesus willingly gave.

In his tender mercy we hear Jesus say: "Today salvation has come into this house ... For the Son of Man came to seek and save what was lost."

Woman caught in adultery

Who can talk about second chances and not mention the woman caught in adultery?

John 8: 3-11 tells how the teachers of the law brought the woman to Jesus.

"In the law, Moses commanded us to stone such women. Now what do you say?" they asked.

Obviously, nobody seemed angry at the man caught with this woman - but she was facing a painful death.

If anybody needed a second chance, she did.

And Jesus gave her one.

"If any one of you is without sin, let him be the first to throw a stone at her," Jesus told the crowd.

One by one, the accusers went away. (I love when I read that the older ones left first. Apparently, age had taught them something.)

After they left, Jesus told the woman that he didn't condemn her, but also that she should leave her life of sin.

She had a second chance. It was up to her to decide what she'd do with it.

As I read these stories I'm reminded of something that Christian author and speaker Joyce Meyer says. Meyer, who was sexually abused as a child, admits she had a rough start.

But, today she says, "It's not how you start, it's how you finish that counts."

That might be a good way to describe Leo the dog. I don't know if he ever killed any dogs in a fight, but I believe he's showing cancer patients that they have a fighting chance. And he's showing kids on probation that there is hope - no matter what their background.

Our God is a God of second chances, ready to help us restore our lives when we earnestly seek him.

As Christians we know that Jesus gave everyone a second chance when he died on the cross.

That's the best second chance of all.

*Note: The Leo story was reported by Marianne Favro of NBC affiliate KNTV of San Francisco and Alex Johnson of msnbc.com. NBC affiliate WAVY of Hampton Roads, Va., contributed to this report.

The God Who Works Things Out

A legion of worries marched through my brain as I sat on the edge of the bed in my motel room.

"How am I going to do this?" I wondered.

I picked up a Bible from the nearby nightstand and tried to push my concerns aside, but it wasn't easy.

It hadn't been a good weekend. It was May 1996, and my dad and I were traveling to western Nebraska to move his belongings from Sidney to Fremont. I would keep them in my garage here (until we bought our own house). Dad had moved into The Lutheran Home in Omaha and wanted me to have the furniture that he and mom had owned for years. After my dad's bouts in the hospital, it would be nice to have him closer to me - and it seemed like we had a plan.

But nothing had gone as planned.

On the way to Sidney, Dad and I stopped at McDonald's in Lexington. When we were ready to leave, we discovered that his car wouldn't start. I called my Aunt Ena who was at dad's house. She and her brother - my Uncle Rick - were trying to clear out the basement - nothing short of a monumental task.

She suggested that I rent a car, but it was Sunday and those places were closed.

I asked a convenience store clerk if anyone would be willing to drive us to Sidney, a few hours away. She recommended a young man from town. The next thing I knew we were on the road.

The young man was friendly and we had a relaxing ride; we paid him for his time and gas.

We were tired when we finally reached Dad's house, but were happy to see my hard-working aunt and uncle.

When a neighbor stopped over to say "hello," we told him our plight. He suggested we call the dealer who had recently sold my dad that car.

In the end, my dad traded his vehicle for a different - and nicer

- car. We just had to go back to Lexington and retrieve the license plates from the old car, now in a mechanic's shop.

My dad and I returned to Lexington the next day. It was early evening by the time we reached our destination. We were going to spend the night in a motel, then get the plates and return to eastern Nebraska in time for my dad's dialysis treatment at Omaha's Clarkson Hospital.

I was tired when we reached the motel, but I couldn't sleep. As I picked up the Bible, I wondered what would go wrong next.

Would we have trouble finding the mechanic's shop? The car that broke down was towed from the restaurant and we'd never been to the repair shop. Would I be able to get Dad back to Omaha in time for his treatment? Would I be exhausted the next day at work?

I shoved those thoughts aside as I opened the Bible and decided to start reading whatever I turned to first. I've often asked God to speak to me through his word, but I can't recall if I prayed those words as I opened the book.

It didn't matter.

I might have forgotten to ask for help, but God didn't forget to supply it.

I turned to the 16th chapter in the book of Mark, which tells about women going to Jesus' tomb to anoint his body as was their custom. On the way, the women were wondering who would roll the heavy stone away from the tomb's door.

But when they reached the tomb, the women found that the stone was rolled aside. Jesus was gone and in his place sat an angel who told them that their Lord had risen from the dead.

I couldn't help but see a parallel between the women's situation and mine. Like me, they were wondering how they were going to solve a problem. Yet when they reached their destination, they discovered that God had worked everything out ahead of time - maybe not how they had expected - but in a much better way.

What began as a problem became a joy and the women became witnesses to an incredible miracle.

The next day, my dad and I found the mechanic's shop, got the license plates and Dad made it to his treatment in time. In the midst of all my worries, I, too, would see our God work everything out. God the planner. God the miracle-maker. God the lover of our souls.

Our greatest and foremost benefactor, now and forever.

As I look back on those days, I'm reminded of the title of a book by the wonderful Christian author Max Lucado. It's called "He Still Moves Stones."

I believe that's true. Does a big stone of fear, grief or regret block your way? God can move it.

I'm also reminded of what the angel told the women: "He is risen. He is not here ... but go and tell his disciples ... He is going ahead of you into Galilee."

Did you notice that the angel told them to go?

They weren't supposed to stay in that dark tomb. Christ wasn't there anymore, so why should they be?

I believe that sends a message to us today.

We're not supposed to linger in the empty tombs of loneliness, doubt and guilt. Jesus has risen. He's not in a dark tomb anymore, so why should we be?

Better yet, he goes ahead of us, just like he did for those women so many years ago.

Now it's our job to follow him and tell others what he's done for us.

And that, after all, we have a God who works things out.

Spiritual Dialysis

I wrote the following column in 1996, years before the weekly Spiritual Spinach column ever came to be. I don't know whatever happened to Maggie Randall, but her example remains a testimony to me even today.

Her name is Maggie Randall.

She is a small cheerful woman who dreams of writing comedy for David Letterman, is quick to start a conversation and doesn't mind sharing her faith.

To me, Maggie is the brightest face in the dialysis unit at Omaha's Clarkson Hospital. I met Maggie while visiting a relative there. And although my relative no longer needs dialysis, Maggie maintains the same thrice-weekly visits. People like Maggie need dialysis when their kidneys cannot filter waste products out of the blood.

Through dialysis, a person's blood is taken - a little at a time - from his or her body. Waste products are removed and then the blood is restored. From what I understand, dialysis means the difference between life and death for a person experiencing kidney failure.

For Maggie, that means spending three hours, three times a week hooked to a dialysis machine. It means she must watch her diet and fluid intake. And it means she tires easily.

Maggie is only 40 years old. She was 20 when her kidneys failed. She had two transplants, one of which was successful from 1976 to 1984. After her body rejected the second kidney, she resumed dialysis.

Some people in Maggie's circumstances might be bitter. Maggie won't indulge herself in that.

"It (bitterness) is negative energy," she says. "I have limited energy anyway, so why use it up in a negative way?"

I'm sure Maggie gets blue occasionally, but I am inspired by her generally positive attitude. I think I can learn a lot from Maggie and I have found an interesting parallel between faith and dialysis.

I've been blessed with healthy kidneys, but I believe I experience a dialysis-type process whenever I go to church. Let me explain. All week long, waste products accumulate in my spiritual system. They may come in the form of anger, bitterness, pride, selfishness or some other failing so common to the human race.

I can't speak for other people, but something happens to me when I go to church. I can see a little bit of myself when the pastor talks about people of Bible times. I seem to share the same impulsiveness that Peter often demonstrated. Like Thomas, I tend to doubt and want to be shown proof of what I cannot see.

Sometime during the sermon, that dialysis seems to take place. For a brief moment, I realize that being angry at someone isn't as important as being right with God, that being bitter seems petty when I consider how much Christ forgives me every day. I try to remember these things throughout the week, but I can be pretty forgetful sometimes. That poison builds up in my system and it's time for spiritual dialysis again.

Now, I don't want to diminish what real dialysis patients live with on a daily basis. They face needles. They deal with sitting in basically one position for three to four hours at a time. And after their treatments, they sometimes battle light-headedness or dizziness or nausea. To me, they are the picture of bravery in the face of adversity. In them, I see the God-given resilience of the human spirit.

I can't begin to know what a real dialysis patient experiences. But I know that some things are as toxic to the soul as waste products are to the body.

I think people need the kind of dialysis that comes from going to church, reading the Bible and praying. Without it, they die spiritually. I also know that they must be consistent.

A nurse once told me that the dialysis machines have only 12 hours each week to perform the same tasks my kidneys do 24 hours a day. In the same way, I think people shouldn't expect one big "house cleaning" at church each week, but also should pray and the read Bible all week long - a continual cleaning of sorts.

I know that's easier said than done. I, too, struggle to make Wednesday night church services, to finish my prayers before falling asleep at night and to remember my daily devotions. But then God gets my attention. He reminds me how fortunate I am to be healthy, and how all Christians are called to tell others about the love of God.

Maggie may not be a pastor, but she has a ministry.

She doesn't give a sermon behind a pulpit. And yet, the simple, quiet truth she speaks from the dialysis room chair is enough to feed the soul.

"God can work through everybody, everywhere," she says, grinning.

As I leave the dialysis unit, I can't help but think that while Maggie's kidneys don't work, her heart is just fine.

A postscript: God has been so gracious. He's grown my faith and hunger for his word to the point where I don't go a day without reading some sort of devotion or spend time in study of his word. My prayer life is growing and my husband and I regularly attend our church Sundays and Wednesdays. I know it's only by his grace that we are able to do any of this. He is truly a good and faithful God.

"A merry heart doeth good like a medicine, but a broken spirit drieth the bones," Proverbs 17:22.

The God Who Seeks Us Out

Pastor Willie Wampler calls it God's top priority:

To share the Gospel with lost and hurting people everywhere.

It's not that church gatherings, fellowship and worship aren't important.

They are.

But they're not No. 1, Wampler says.

When Wampler came to my church quite some time ago, he showed a video of what looks like a homeless man digging in a dumpster. In the video, the man later sits on a curb and plays an accordion while precious few people drop a coin or two in his paper cup. The curbside musician pauses briefly and pulls a newspaper obituary from his pocket. He looks at it, then reaches for something else.

But it isn't there.

Frantically, he searches through his things. He races from one dumpster to another trying to find it. Briefly, he turns around to see someone running off with his accordion. Maybe someone grabbed his cup of coins, too, but he doesn't care. He keeps searching.

Then he finds it: a beautiful necklace.

His memory suddenly takes him back to a different place. He is placing the necklace on a pretty little blonde who was probably his daughter - most likely the person whose obituary he carries.

Suddenly, the man is happy. Not because he's lost someone precious, but because he's found the necklace that reminds him of her.

In the end, he smiles as he sits on the curb.

He is at peace, having found that which is most dear to him.

The touching video is a picture of God, Wampler said.

Then Wampler reminded his listeners of some of Jesus' stories, called parables. In the first, a woman loses one of her 10 silver coins. She lights a lamp, sweeps the house and searches carefully until she finds it. When she does, she's overjoyed.

In another parable, Jesus asks this question: Suppose a man has 100 sheep and loses one of them?

"Does he not leave the 99 in the open country and go after the lost sheep until he finds it? And when he finds it, he joyfully puts it on his shoulders and goes home."

The man then calls his friends and neighbors together to rejoice.

"I tell you that in the same way there will be more rejoicing in heaven over one sinner who repents than over 99 righteous persons who do not need to repent," Jesus says.

The stories illustrate how important people are to God.

Yet how can people know about the Gospel if they haven't heard it?

Well, surely everyone in America has heard about
Jesus, right?

Maybe not.

Wampler said 50 percent of the people in this country don't know who Jesus is.

Sound like a lot? Perhaps, but with our ever-changing, ever-growing society, Wampler might not be far off.

I have similarly discovered that while many people may have heard of Jesus, they know little about the Bible. I also talked to one woman, who was in her 30s and said she'd never stepped foot in a church until the week before I met her.

I've known incredibly intelligent, well-read, knowledgeable people who don't know simple Bible stories. Trust me when I tell you these people could really put me to shame with all the other facts they know.

And just so I don't sound like some spiritual giant, let me tell you that I was 16 years old before someone explained to me what the Gospel was really all about.

The pastor simply said we're all sinners (nobody's perfect) and that sin separates us from God.

So first, we need to pray to God and repent of our sins - that means to be so sorry for our sins that we never want to do them again and to turn away from them. Then we must believe that Jesus died on the cross to save us from our sins - and rose again from the dead. Christ paid the price so we don't have to. We then ask Jesus to come into our hearts and be our savior. After that - when we die - we will go to heaven forever.

I served Jesus faithfully for a while after I prayed that prayer and gave my life to him, but then I slipped away and made some poor choices.

You might say that I became part of Christ's top priority. He then surrounded me with Christian friends and I came back to serving him.

I guess I was a sheep that was lost.

But he found me.

Coming in the Front Door

If you've ever worked with the public, then you know there are some hard-to-deal with customers.

But then there are those you really like to see come in the door.

I miss some of the people who once walked through the front door of the Fremont Tribune.

Harold Bausch and his wife, Lil, were square dancers. Harold often brought in news about the Starlighters Square Dance Club. He was friendly and always had a kind word.

There was smiling Gertrude Haidley with her garden club news and Bob Morton who used to run the Cinema III Theatre on 23rd Street.

Bob, who'd bring in his little dog, liked to tell me that the Richard Pryor/Gene Wilder movie "Silver Streak" was so popular it played for 13 weeks at the theater. "Three Men and a Baby," which starred Tom Selleck and Ted Danson, almost beat that record with 12.

I always enjoyed seeing Emil Mares. Did you know he flew a glider during the D-Day invasion of Normandy in World War II? The glider crash landed and Emil was injured, but a Polish woman, who was a forced laborer, hid him under a pile of manure, where the Nazis wouldn't look. She kept moving Emil until she got him to the American forces at St. Mere Eglis. He then was put on a hospital ship bound for England.

Decades after the war, Emil would come to my desk with news of the Red Cross blood drives. Positive and professional, he always seemed to appreciate us putting the notices in the newspaper. Today, Dodge County's Red Cross chapter even has an award named for him.

In my own heart, Emil deserves a special tribute, because I remember how he stopped by my dad's room at Omaha's Clarkson Hospital. My dad was so hard of hearing - and didn't have his hearing aid with him - that I had to write down what Emil was trying to say on a piece of paper and let my father read it.

Despite the communication problem, I know my dad, also a World War II veteran, was so pleased and honored to meet Emil.

There are other people who I'm probably forgetting, but I certainly would be remiss in not mentioning Dorrie Dugan.

Dorrie brought in news about Jobs Daughters. She also brought us articles about Boys and Girls State. Since there were winners and alternates from both Fremont High and Bergan Catholic schools, she'd carefully tape the students' school photos on white cardboard with their names written underneath to prevent confusion. I don't know how many years we ran stories about that, but I know that lots of kids have Dorrie to thank for having their photo in with the article.

Occasionally, Dorrie and I would go to lunch and she'd ask me about my work and family. She came to my wedding and once took a picture of my two sons. When my dad died, she was one of the very first people I called. Her son, Bill, owns Lattin-Dugan-Chambers Funeral Home and we made arrangements for a service in Fremont and then for my dad to be transported to western Nebraska for burial.

The day of my dad's funeral was tough.

Dorrie and her daughter-in-law, Jane, attended my father's Fremont service. That was nice since my dad didn't know too many people here.

Years passed and occasionally I'd see Dorrie. I remember one afternoon when I saw Jane in a grocery store parking lot and asked how Dorrie was. She said I should just come with her and visit Dorrie right then.

I should know better, but I always seem to think I'll have another chance. I didn't visit Dorrie that day.

I didn't get another chance.

That makes me sad and I hate the way that death robs us of people we care about.

Somehow, though, I think God views death a little differently than we do. I'm reminded of the verse, Psalm 116:15, which reads, "Precious in the sight of the Lord is the death of his saints."

In reading this verse, I picture a merciful God watching tenderly as his beloved child slips from life on this earth to life in a better place.

I think humans see death as an end, where God sees it as a beginning. We see it as a closed door. He sees it as a bridge.

I don't know where he got this saying, but perhaps the Rev. Nathan Ennis said it best when he spoke at my dad's funeral. He said, "Death is not a period. It's only a comma."

I've thought about that and many other things when I've pondered heaven and eternal life.

Now, I don't know if heaven has a door. But I'd like to think that when I come in, I will see people I haven't seen in a very long time - people I've missed.

And just as I looked up from my work to see a friendly face come in through the Tribune's front door, I hope that my brothers and sisters in Christ will look up and notice someone they really like - someone who will come in and share a bit of good news with them.

A Butterfly Story

Some time ago a friend of mine, Cheryl Warren, married her fiance, the Rev. Mike Anderson.

The wedding was lovely. The bride was radiant and both she and the groom looked very happy.

But one of the things that struck me most was the sermon.

Really.

During the sermon, the Rev. Richard Brian told a story about a man and a butterfly. He quoted Jeff Schreve, pastor of First Baptist Church in Texarkana, Texas, as the author. I've also seen different versions of the story on the Internet.

Basically it goes like this:

A man found a cocoon of a butterfly and one day a small opening appeared. He watched the butterfly struggle for several hours to force its body through the tiny opening.

At one point, it seemed to stop making progress.

So the man decided to help the butterfly. Taking a pair of scissors, he cut off the rest of the cocoon.

The butterfly emerged easily.

But something was wrong.

It had a small swollen body and shriveled wings. The man thought that eventually the butterfly would be able to fly - but that never happened.

What the man, in his haste and pity, didn't understand was that the butterfly needed to struggle. As a butterfly struggles to get through the cocoon, a fluid from its body is forced onto the wings, making them strong and ready for flight.

The point is that as humans, we sometimes need struggles, too. If God never allowed any struggles or obstacles for us to overcome, we wouldn't be very strong or compassionate people.

In his sermon, the Methodist pastor also pointed out that a butterfly has a less-than-enviable life. It begins as a small egg deposited on a leaf. The egg hatches into a caterpillar, which eventually makes a cocoon.

Throughout the process, it is very vulnerable. At any time, it can be stepped on or eaten or meet with some other deathly fate. If it does survive and make its way from the cocoon, it lives a rather solitary life. Although surrounded by a multitude of other butterflies, its life is mainly a solo event.

"A butterfly does not huddle with another butterfly when it is cold; a butterfly, like a twig, is easily broken; a butterfly has no one to turn to in times of trouble; no one to hold its' hands when it is sad; no one to share its day with," the pastor said.

I think that's true.

Whether married or single, we all need people who will stay by us through good times and bad.

The Old Testament book of Ecclesiastes perhaps says it best. In the fourth chapter, this very interesting book of the Bible says: "Two are better than one, because they have a good return for their work;

"If one falls down, his friend can help him up. But pity the man who falls and has no one to help him up!

"Also, if two lie down together, they will keep warm. But how can one keep warm alone?

"Though one may be overpowered, two can defend themselves.

A cord of three strands is not quickly broken."

To me that cord is a picture of how a marriage should be: the husband, the wife and God - three strands which make up one very strong bond. I believe our marriages can survive when we truly put God at the center.

Why?

Maybe it's because after several years of marriage, we might not always feel like taking out the trash, washing piles of laundry or running some errand so our spouse won't have to.

And I think that's where God comes in. While we might not feel like doing it for our spouse, we do it because we know it will please God. Then - in the process of pleasing God - we show love to our spouse.

Those acts of love can add up. And even if a spouse doesn't always notice, God does and I believes he rewards his children for it.

I also believe we avoid a multitude of pitfalls when we obey God's word. And I think we can better withstand life's storms if we hold on tight to each other and God - and seek his direction.

I wish my dear friend Cheryl and her new husband, Mike, all the happiness in the world. I know their marriage will be God-centered and not self-centered and that they will show the Lord's love to others.

And I'll bet that when their grandchildren ask them about marriage, they'll tell them a story about butterflies.

Film, Fruit and the Holy Spirit

Do you own a digital camera?

The Tribune has a couple and I like them. I can take a photo of someone, then look on the camera's little screen to see if I like the picture or need to take another. When I get back to work, I can download the image right into the computer and have a photo for the newspaper.

Times sure have changed.

When I started working at the Tribune in 1981, we only had cameras that used film. We'd take photos and then our photographer would undergo the labor intensive process of developing the black and white film and making prints.

I learned how to develop film in college. It's not that fun. After all these years, the process is a little fuzzy - much like the images in my early photographs. But the basic procedure is this:

* Open the film canister in a dark room.

* Put the film on a metal or plastic reel. That's not easy to do in the dark. You have to be careful, because if one part of the film touches another it can ruin a picture.

* Put the film in a little metal tank with a lid and add a chemical to develop the film.

* When the developing is done, run water into the tank to stop the process.

* Add a fixer.

* Hang negatives up to dry.

I won't even go into how we made prints - one by one - which also involved a developer, stop bath, fixer and drying process.

The point is: It took time.

A lot of things take time. Like developing spiritually. There's no such thing as instant spiritual maturity. Learning to trust God through difficult times is a process for most of us. Learning to be kind, loving and patient during infuriating - or even irritating - situations doesn't come naturally.

Don't believe me?

Think how you feel (and react) the next time someone turns right in front of you in traffic. Or when your child won't stop crying in a grocery store. Or when someone snaps at you.

It's not so easy to be kind. But Christian author and speaker Joyce Meyer says when we give our hearts to Christ and are filled with the Holy Spirit we gain what's called the fruit of the spirit.

What's this fruit?

The book of Galatians, chapter 5 in the Bible tells us. The fruit of the spirit is: love, joy, peace, patience, kindness, goodness, faithfulness, gentleness and self-control.

Just like you can see fruit on a tree, people can tell when you love God, are trying to do what he says and he's working in your life.

When you stay calm rather than honking your horn at the guy in traffic or yelling at your child in the store or telling off the person who snapped at you - that's the fruit of the spirit working in you.

And people notice.

Aw c'mon, you say, nobody's perfect.

You're right. We're not. We all have our moments. We get mad and jealous and worried and impatient.

And I think so many Christians get frustrated because they try to be good, loving and patient in their own strength.

But we can't do it in our own strength. We need to ask God to help us.

Here are some things I've prayed:

"God, please help me to be the person - the servant - you want me to be."

"God, please give me your love, your peace, your kindness .... help me to love and trust you."

"God, please help me. I can't do this on my own."

I gained so much peace when I quit trying to do everything in my own strength. Just like a car needs gas to run, we need the Holy Spirit to flow through us and help us be what God needs us to be - loving people for a hurting world.

But becoming those people takes time. Or, at least, it has for me - and it's a continuing process.

Meyer also says the fruit takes time to develop. To illustrate, she takes pictures with a film camera. Where are the pictures? In the camera. They just need to be developed.

And they're developed in a dark room.

Similarly, the fruit of the spirit is developed in the dark room of life's trials, she says.

I think that's true.

With the help of the Holy Spirit, we can develop patience while we're waiting for that report from the doctor or kindness when we have to deal with a troublesome customer or gentleness when we have to confront someone who's going down the wrong road of life.

We have to do our part. We have to try - always leaning on God, who's a real master at this kind of stuff.

When we do, I believe people will see the good fruit. They'll see snapshots of our lives that hopefully will bring them closer to our loving God.

Looking back, I'm really glad that I don't have to develop film or make prints. I don't miss being in the college darkroom at 2 a.m., trying to finish a project for the next day.

But I don't think I'd appreciate today's technology nearly so much if I hadn't had to deal with the film.

And maybe I wouldn't appreciate God's peace, love and gentleness if I hadn't known worry, rejection and harshness.

It's an appreciation that took time to develop.

The God Who Loves Underdogs

I have a song stuck in my head.

It's "I Dreamed A Dream" from Les Miserables. I first heard it when a morning news show aired a segment about a Scottish woman named Susan Boyle.

Boyle had just appeared on "Britain's Got Talent," the overseas version of "America's Got Talent."

Normally, I'm hurrying around in the morning trying to get ready for work, but the song - and Susan - stopped me in my tracks.

Susan is an unemployed, 47-year-old church volunteer, who lives alone with her cat, Pebbles. Never married - and never even been kissed - Susan cared for her parents until their deaths. As a child, she was picked on at school, yet you couldn't tell it by her spunky on-stage demeanor.

She came out and stood before judges Simon Cowell, Piers Morgan and the very pretty blonde Amanda Holden. Susan smiled at her judges and the audience, but you could almost feel the skepticism rise in the crowd.

You see, Susan doesn't look like the posh celebrities that the world has grown used to. She's a chunky woman with curly, graying hair that appears to be thinning at the crown of her head. No waxed eyebrows on this girl. No long, polished nails. No designer duds. Instead she wore a simple, light yellow dress, the type your grandma might wear to church some Sundays.

But Susan had confidence in her abilities. And when Cowell rolled his eyes after hearing her age, she said "that's just one side of me" and shifted her hips back and forth then nodded her head as if to say "So there!"

Perhaps going by the title of her song, Cowell asked what Susan's dream was. Audience members flashed that "you've got to be kidding look" when Susan announced that she wants to be a professional singer. Cowell appeared annoyed and bored as the music began.

Then something absolutely wonderful happened.

Susan started to sing.

And it was breathtakingly beautiful. She barely got out a few words before the crowd began to cheer wildly. Cowell's eyebrows shot up like fireworks. Pretty Amanda's jaw dropped and Piers seemed genuinely touched.

After a short time, Amanda's eyes looked a bit teary.

And Cowell?

He had a smile as wide as Texas as he sat there, like a dreamy-eyed schoolboy, with his head in his hands. Audience members stood, cheered and clapped their hands over their heads as the camera panned the crowd.

As I stood there, staring at the TV (and later watching it repeatedly on YouTube), I almost felt as if I were watching the end of a beautiful movie where an underdog becomes a winner and a hero.

The audience roared even louder as the lovely music and Susan's voice reached a crescendo. Then, far too soon, the song ended. Piers and Amanda were on their feet, clapping.

Piers told how surprised he was by Susan's incredible performance. Amanda said how cynical people had been, what a wake-up call they'd had, and how much of a privilege it was to hear Susan sing.

All the judges gave her the green light to go on to the next round of competition and the very elated Susan stamped her feet in delight.

Since then, people have compared her story to fairy tales and Disney movies. Indeed, it seems like a dream come true and such a reminder of how people really can't judge a book by its cover.

I almost get teary-eyed thinking about it.

I love the thought of a very average-looking woman all but knocking over an audience with her talent, finally being recognized after so many years in what probably was virtual oblivion. And as a rather ordinary-looking woman, myself, who knows the dull pain of being picked on at school and overlooked at dances as a young person, there's something very rich about seeing another common-looking woman getting her time in the spotlight.

And believe it or not, it makes me think about Jesus.

Now, I assume that most of us imagine our Lord and Savior as a very handsome man - with our mental images based on lovely portraits that depict him with blue eyes, finely chiseled features and long, flowing light brown hair.

But I seriously doubt that he looked much like that. Just take a look at how he is described in the Old Testament book of Isaiah.

The passages can be found in chapter 53, starting in the middle of verse 2: "....He had no beauty or majesty to attract us to him, nothing in his appearance that we should desire him."

Did you catch that?

"He had no beauty or majesty."

The Message Bible says it like this: "There was nothing attractive about him, nothing to cause us to take a second look. He was looked down on and passed over."*

I truly believe that Jesus was quite common looking. Physically, it doesn't sound like he stood out in a crowd.

Oh, but spiritually?

That was another story. He truly was a head and shoulders above the rest; the son of God who demonstrated beauty - not in how he looked - but in what he did.

Can you just see him healing the sick? Comforting the fearful? Tenderly including those shunned by society?

Beautiful acts by an ordinary-looking Savior. I love the thought of that. What's more, I find comfort in a Savior who can relate to those of us who have ever felt plain or passed over.

I truly hope that Susan Boyle's dreams are fulfilled. And as the song she sang replays in my brain, I continue to think how very good our God is. He makes winners, heroes and champions out of ordinary people. Don't believe me? Just read the stories of Gideon, David and Joseph in the Bible, then think of modern-day people like Susan. It's true. He lifts the downtrodden and gives grace to the humble.

And even if the rest of the world looks the other way, he never overlooks an underdog.

A postscript: Susan Boyle placed second in the competition, behind a dance troupe, called "Diversity." However, I read where the YouTube segment of Susan's performance had reached 100 million hits and, since then, I've heard that it was twice that number. Whatever happens, she has made her mark.

* Scripture taken from The Message. Copyright - 1993, 1994, 1995, 1996, 2000, 2001, 2002. Used by permission of NavPress Publishing Group."

Burn Treatments

If you've ever been burned, you know how painful it can be.

One of my loved ones was burned in an accident not long ago. We took him to the University of Nebraska Medical Center's burn center and watched as a nurse wiped a wet, soapy towel over the burned areas. Next, she popped the blisters and a doctor carefully trimmed away the damaged skin.

It was a painful process for the patient to endure and for us to watch. The nurse and doctor applied the dressings and our loved one went home. As time progressed, he began to heal.

The situation made me wonder about something: How many times are people burned - not physically, but emotionally and spiritually - by something someone said.

Or did?

Or didn't do?

And instead of those burns being treated, they're left to fester.

Oh, these walking wounded try to cover their burns. They say things like: "I really don't care," "It doesn't matter anymore" or "That jerk will get it some day."

But like a thin, see-through gauze, their comments can't hide the burn that lies beneath.

Day after day. Month after month. And sometimes year after year, they pass through life with pain they think nobody sees.

Yet their lives are infected by the complications of that burn.

Infection was one of the things the burn center nurses repeatedly warned us about. I even discussed that with Dr. Debra Reilly, a plastic surgeon and medical director of the burn center.

She told me that infection alters blood flow to the localized burn. A second-degree burn may turn into a third-degree burn. The burn can then take longer to heal - thus resulting in prolonged pain and more scarring.

That infection can even get into the bloodstream and make the person sick all over.

As I consider this, I wonder how many people are suffering from emotional and spiritual infections like: anger, resentment, unforgiveness, bitterness, despair, discouragement and cynicism.

How many just feel sick all over and wonder why?

That's why I think it's so important that these burns be treated. Just as we took our loved one to a burn center, filled with educated, trained and experienced people, I think spiritually burned victims sometimes need to seek professionals, too. But before seeing a professional, I truly believe these patients-in-waiting need to pray - and earnestly seek God - about whom they should go to.

My personal preference is a qualified, Christian pastor or counselor, who has the tools, knowledge and experience needed to help someone with a deep, spiritual burn.

And just like treating a physical burn can be painful, the same can be true for a spiritual or emotional burn. The person may not want to even have anyone look at his burn.

But what if my loved one had refused the show his burns to the doctor? What if he'd said, "No it's too ugly. It's too hideous. I don't want you to see it."

How would the doctor and nurses ever have treated those burns?

In the same way, a spiritually burned person may be ashamed of his wound, may think it looks too grotesque for anyone else to see. But exposing that burn and its severity is the first step to treatment.

And the wonderful thing about treatment is that it can allow for healing.

Reilly told me how an antibiotic ointment is applied to burns. And after my loved one started to heal, he reached a point where he only needed a water-based lotion.

Did you catch that?

Water-based lotion.

Whenever I think of water, I think of Jesus Christ who is our living water.

Who better than Jesus to salve and soothe our burns? Who better than our loving God to bring healing and wholeness?

It's true that a good professional can help treat the burn, but only God actually brings the healing - if we let him.

It all starts with a single step: a cry to the only one who can really help any of us.

As Psalms 147:3 in the Bible says: "He heals the brokenhearted and binds up their wounds."

Sounds like some good spiritual first aid to me.

A postscript: Once a patient has been burned, it's important for her to drink fluids to help replace what was lost.

Reilly said, however, that these fluids need to contain electrolytes, some sugar and some protein to replace the serum being leaked out of the open burned skin.

Similarly, I believe that when a person is burned spiritually, he needs to drink deeply from the word of God. While other secular literature certainly may help some, I truly believe that nothing can replenish what was lost like God's word - which contains the spiritual electrolytes we need.

Seeking Direction

I am directionally challenged.

Perhaps one of the best examples occurred many years ago when I was a young reporter. I came into work that morning and my editors sent me out to a hog confinement fire. On the way, however, I met with a road construction detour. I followed the detour and thought I'd still find the place, but something went wrong.

I stopped at a farmhouse to get directions. No one was home. I stopped at another place and the young woman who answered the door acted as if she was scared of me.

Maybe I forgot to put on makeup that morning. Or maybe a somewhat frenzied stranger was alarming to her.

Anyway, she wasn't sure where the farm was. There went my theory that farm people all know each other.

I started along yet another gravel road when I saw a firetruck headed my way. I frantically waved my hand back and forth, hoping he'd stop and give me some information or directions or something.

The driver just waved back.

He probably thought I was the friendliest motorist he'd come across that day.

By the time I found the farm, the fire was out. I felt sorry for the people who were sorting through things and barely seemed to notice my late arrival. I took some photos of the charred remains and returned to work.

My editors weren't impressed with my after-the-fire photos.

Now please keep in mind that this was in the day before cell phones, Global Positioning Satellite devices and those green county road signs with numbers and alphabet letters. It wasn't like I had a lot of help out there.

Life is kind of like that, though.

How many times do we wish we had a big sign from God saying: "Go this way. Turn here. Make a right"?

I envied the Israelites recently when I had a rather big decision to make.

After God freed the Israelites from slavery in Egypt, he went ahead of them in a pillar of cloud by day to guide them and a pillar of fire by night to give them light.

They could travel by day or night.

In the Bible, the book of Numbers gives even more detail in chapter nine, starting with verse 15. Written by the Israelite leader Moses, the account tells how the cloud covered the tabernacle (what you might call a portable church-type structure). When the cloud lifted above the tabernacle, the Israelites set out across the desert. Wherever the cloud settled, they encamped.

If the cloud remained a long time, even for a year, the Israelites stayed put. If the cloud remained only two days - then moved - they set out.

Now in chapter 10 we learn that Moses did ask his brother-in-law, a non-Israelite, to accompany them and show them the best places to camp.

You might call him an ancient-day tour guide.

I could have used a pillar of cloud or a tour guide that day I tried to find the hog confinement fire.

And I sure wished I had a pillar of cloud as I tried to make my way through a wilderness of indecision recently. I even remember praying, "Please God, give me a pillar of cloud, a pillar of fire - a pillar of peanut butter and jelly sandwiches - anything to tell me which way to go and what to do!"

But I didn't get a pillar.

Instead, I ended up talking to a Christian woman about my situation. She told me that God doesn't always give us a pillar. Sometimes he just gives us a gentle nudge.

I believe that nudge comes via the Holy Spirit.

Just take a look at the book of John in the Bible. It tells about a discussion Jesus had with his disciples before he died on the cross. In chapter 14, verse 26, he said: "But the counselor, the Holy Spirit, whom the father will send in my name will teach you all things and will remind you of everything I have said to you."

We may not have a pillar of cloud, but we have the Holy Spirit and the Bible.

As I prayed about the situation, certain options were eliminated. Eventually, I knew what I was going to do. Everything just started to fall into place.

I don't know if I got that nudge - although I've had that in the past - but I did have peace about the direction I was taking. And sometimes, I think peace isn't so much of an overwhelming feeling as it is just the absence of turmoil.

Anyway, I've set out on my own little journey; it's going to be an adventure.

And I know that with God leading the way, I can't go wrong.

Or get lost.

That's good news for a directionally challenged person like myself.

A postscript: Persistence in prayer is important. Don't give up if you don't immediately see an answer. Remember what Christ said in the book of Matthew, chapter 7, verse 7 in the Bible: "Ask and it will be given to you; seek and you will find; knock and the door will be opened to you. For everyone who asks, receives; he who seeks finds; and to him who knocks, the door will be opened."

Other comforting Scriptures: "Call to me and I will answer you and tell you great and unsearchable things you do not know." Jeremiah 33:3.

"Whether you turn to the right or to the left, your ears will hear a voice behind you, say: 'This is the way, walk in it.'" Isaiah 30:21.

Zip Line Zoe

A word of caution: The 10th paragraph of this column may be very difficult, or even traumatic, for someone who's ever suffered abuse to read. Someone suffering from Post Traumatic Stress Syndrome due to sexual abuse may need to skip that paragraph.

He calls her "Zip Line Zoe."

That's not her real name, but the Rev. Scott Murrish can't divulge the real names of children who come to Royal Family Kids Camps each year.

Scott is a regional field representative for the non-profit organization that provides weeklong summer camps for abused, neglected and abandoned children.

Zoe was a 9-year-old girl who attended a camp in Nebraska. And Scott, a former Fremont pastor, usually tells her story when he speaks to groups.

He begins by telling how her laughter filled the air and her long red hair flowed in the breeze as she sailed to the bottom of a three-story zip line at camp. Her counselor and her camp buddy applauded when she reached her goal.

Scott walked up to Zoe as she started to unbuckle her safety harness and remove her helmet. He noticed how much fun she was having and had a question for her:

"What's your favorite part about kids camp?" he asked.

Now Scott was expecting her to say that she liked the swimming or the music or fun times outdoors.

But she didn't say any of those things.

Instead, she looked up at him with her big green eyes and said: "My favorite thing is that I have a safe bed to sleep in. At home, my stepdad used to come into my room and do things to me at night. I had to pretend to be asleep, otherwise I would get in big trouble. That doesn't happen at kids camp. Everyone here is safe."

Scott was stunned.

"I know that all the kids at Royal Family Kids Camps have gone through horrific times of abuse, but this beautiful little redhead stopped me cold," he said.

Without skipping a beat, Zoe, her counselor and camp buddy ran off to the waterfront to go swimming.

Scott's head was still swimming by what he heard, but it was a reminder of why these camps are important.

"Kids' lives are reshaped because they're given a week of unconditional love and shown that they can be successful and have hope for a positive future," he said.

What good does one week - out of an entire year - do for a child?

"Lives are changed not in a week, but in a moment," he said. "One positive memory can have a lifetime impact on the heart of a child."

Scott compares the weeklong camps to the North Platte canteen, where townspeople served sandwiches, coffee and pie to servicemen headed to battle in World War II. As troop trains stopped in the Nebraska community, some 6 million soldiers were treated to 10 to 15 minutes of friendship and encouragement along with the food. Those few minutes of kindness would sustain men in foxholes and on front lines.

"The local people literally changed the face of World War II," Scott said, "because soldiers on the front lines would say, 'Do you remember how that food tasted in North Platte and how much those people loved us?' Those positive memories gave them the courage and endurance to make it through the heat of battle."

Scott believes evidence of the camps' success can be seen in numbers of former campers who come back and serve as volunteers.

He also tells the story of the day he was in a restaurant when a young woman, who was the hostess, noticed the logo on his shirt. She said she'd attended the camp for three years in a row and didn't know where she'd be without the love she'd found there.

"I lived in 22 different foster homes and found out that I could be an OK person from my experience at your camp," she said.

Scott anticipates even more stories as increasing numbers of young campers grow into adulthood.

He also compares their stories to Joseph in Old Testament. This Joseph was sold into slavery by his own brothers and later went to prison for a crime he didn't commit. But God would elevate this same Joseph to the position of second in command in Egypt, where he would save many people from famine.

Scott believes the Joseph story shows that these children's lives can be restored.

And that "they can rise to a place of significance in their lives."

In 2009, more than 150 camps are being held in the United States and 20 in foreign countries.

Six camps are scheduled in Nebraska this year in Kearney, Hastings, Lincoln, Grand Island and Columbus. In 2010, camps will be conducted in Fremont and Valentine.

Scott looks forward to these camps, which he knows can help children.

And there are lots of children who need help.

"There are thousands of children (over 3 million reports annually) who navigate a minefield of fear in their own homes, not knowing if the next thing they touch, word they say, or even look they give, will trigger the next violent explosion of pain," Scott said. "Royal Family Kids Camps exist to create positive memories for these hurting children and to give them hope of a brighter future."

Sounds a lot like a verse from the Bible.

It's Jeremiah 29:11 which states: "For I know the plans I have for you, declares the Lord of hosts, plans to prosper and not harm you, plans to give you hope and a future."

That's a verse children, like Zoe, can really cling to.

A portion of the proceeds from this book will go to Royal Family Kids Camps. For more information about this nationwide program or to donate, contact:

Royal Family Kids' Camps, Inc.
3000 W. McArthur Blvd. Suite 412
Santa Ana, CA 92704

www.RFKC.org

The Great Stone Face

"The Great Stone Face."

I've heard that title since I was a child - usually as a joke, referring to someone who had a staid, expressionless face. You may have heard it, too: "Joe just sat there like The Great Stone Face."

Not in any way complimentary.

But when I was in eighth grade we read a shortened version of the story in English class and I've read the entire piece since.

Written by Nathaniel Hawthorne, "The Great Stone Face" is the story of a man, named Ernest - who since childhood - has gazed upon a natural formation of mountainside rock that resembles a human face.

As a boy, Ernest learns a legend which states that someday a child will be born who will become the greatest and most noble person of his time. When this boy reaches manhood, his face will exactly resemble that mountainside image.

Ernest grows up to be a mild-mannered, intelligent and loving person, who dreams about meeting the marvelous man who will resemble the mountain visage.

A very rich man comes along, whom everyone assumes must surely be the one and Ernest hopes this well-heeled merchant will bless others with his wealth. But when he spots the man, Ernest can't see any resemblance at all - and this man, who shows little pity for the poor, himself dies in poverty.

Next comes a great commander, but again Ernest sees no resemblance. Then comes an eloquent and successful statesman, seeking to ride his wave of popularity to the top, caring little if he'd actually benefit anyone else. But poor Ernest can't see any resemblance in this man, either.

In the meantime, hopeful, kind Ernest spends his life blessing his neighbors and growing in wisdom. Eventually, people begin coming from far and wide to hear what this gentle, sincere and wise man has to say.

And whenever Ernest faces disappointment, in his heart he can imagine the benign stone face telling him not to fear - that the man he wants to meet will come.

One day a fine poet arrives to see Ernest, who hopes that this man of literature will resemble the Great Stone Face. But as lovely as the man's words are, the poet knows he hasn't always lived up to what he's written about and, again, Ernest sees no resemblance.

Yet when Ernest speaks, his words have depth, because his life has been one of holy love and good deeds.

Suddenly, the poet realizes something: Ernest bears the very likeness of the Great Stone Face. But, in true humility, Ernest simply goes home, hoping that a wiser and better man than himself will come along.

I was a young woman when I read the full version of that story.

My heart was filled with such hope, but one thing was missing: the mention of God. Although it talks about angels several times, it seemed to reach a certain height and then stop.

However I did notice one thing: Ernest spent his life trying to imitate the man represented by the stone face.

Maybe that's why I think we can learn a lot from Ernest.

Just as he spent every day trying follow what he thought was his stony role model's example, we also can spend each day striving to imitate our great and wonderful role model: Jesus Christ.

Better yet, we don't have to imagine what our Lord wants; his will for our lives is expressed in his word.

How does he want us to live? Take a look through the Gospels. See Jesus sticking up for the underdog? Comforting the poor? Teaching people about God's love wherever he went?

Then look at Matthew, chapter 22, verses 34-39 in the Bible. This is where a Pharisee asks Jesus which is the greatest commandment.

Jesus then says: "Love the Lord your God with all your heart, with all your soul, and with all your mind. This is the greatest commandment. And the second is like it: Love your neighbor as yourself."

Two easy rules. Kind of a CliffsNotes version of love.

So many days I've prayed that God will help me do to just this. I think it's OK to ask God to help me to love him and others, because in myself I know I don't do it very well.

And guess what? Little by little, he's been helping me.

A few weeks ago, my pastor asked our congregation to think about what we might want to have written on our gravestones.

I'm sure many people would want to be listed as a loving mom or dad or a person of honesty and integrity or a person of prayer.

It didn't take me long to decide.

On my gravestone, I hope they write: "She loved her God very well."

If I can do that, I think everything else will fall into place.

Help for Problems, Big and Small

One night, not long ago, I was tossing and turning, trying to get to sleep.

I was facing a situation the next day that if not handled well could end up in a mess.

Angry, frustrated thoughts whirled through my brain.

Why couldn't someone else handle these things? Wasn't it about time for someone else to step up to the plate? Why was it always me?

In the course of world events, it was a very small thing.

But it was bugging me.

So I started talking to God.

Now, I've heard that you should just tell God what's on your mind. And be honest. He knows what you're thinking anyway.

So I did.

Yet as I filed one complaint after another, I started thinking about what Jesus went through before he died on the cross.

The horrible, bloody beating.

The mockery.

The crown of thorns that soldiers jammed on his head.

Suddenly, my problem seemed so pathetically miniscule.

Who was I to complain about anything?

I remembered a Scripture in the Bible. It's found in the book of Luke, chapter 9, verse 23.

In this situation, Christ is talking to his disciples - but the message is for us today, too.

Jesus said: "If anyone would come after me, he must deny himself and take up his cross daily and follow me."

That word, "daily," always gets to me.

And carry a cross?

As the old saying goes, "We all have our crosses to bear" - those situations we'd rather not deal with, but instead must handle the way we know God would want us to.

I apologized to God for my bad attitude. I told God that I didn't wanted to displease him. I wanted to obey him.

I was just tired and needed a break.

Then, a spirit-inspired thought came to me:

Even Jesus had help carrying his cross.

Do you remember this part of the story?

It's found in Luke, chapter 23, verse 26. It tells about Jesus being taken to his death.

It reads: "As they led him away, they seized Simon from Cyrene, who was on his way in from the country, and put the cross on him and made him carry it behind Jesus."

The book of John tells about Jesus carrying his own cross, but at that point he was obviously in such bad shape that he couldn't do it anymore.

I wasn't anywhere near that condition, but I learned long ago that the God who has numbered the hairs on our heads is concerned about our problems - big and small.

So I told God that I'd carry my cross - I just needed a little help.

That help came the next day while I was talking to a friend, who made an amazingly simple suggestion - which I followed.

The situation worked out and seems to be continuing to do so.

After that, I started looking up verses about help in the Bible.

There are several such as:

"We wait in hope for the Lord; he is our help and shield," Psalm 33:20.

And:

"God is our refuge and strength, an ever-present help in trouble," Psalm 45:1.

And:

"The Lord is my strength and my shield; my heart trusts in him, and I am helped," Psalm 28:7

Did you notice how many times the words "strength" and

"shield" are used with the word, "help"?

God helps, protects and strengthens us in many ways - and in many different types of situations.

The key, I believe, is asking him for help.

I didn't start seeing some relief from my internal struggle until after I sought help.

Granted, I think it can take some time for help to arrive.

But just because we don't see anything happening right away, doesn't mean God isn't working behind the scenes, straightening out tangled, troubled situations and softening hearts - including ours - if we let him.

I noticed that I slept a whole lot better the night after I prayed that troubled prayer and then experienced God's help.

And I probably would have gotten even more sleep, if I hadn't stayed up late starting this column.

Middle Management

If you've ever been caught in the middle of an uncomfortable situation, you know how squishy - or even crushing - it can be.

Ask anybody who's caught in the middle of an argument between two friends.

Or two feuding relatives.

Or an unhappy customer and an unrelenting employer.

Years ago, my husband, Chuck, worked for a place that really should have been built with larger air conditioning units.

Customers had some heated words for my maintenance-man husband when they didn't think their living quarters were cooling off well enough.

The poor man did what he could.

But there wasn't much he could do.

Consequently, it almost looked like he wasn't very good at his job.

That was tough.

Worse yet, he was forbidden to say anything about the real problem.

He was caught in the middle.

Now, anyone in middle management can probably tell you similar stories. They get caught in between bosses who want tough jobs done in a certain way and workers who may not want to do them.

Middle managers get stuck between companies that don't think employees need to know every detail and workers who wonder why they have to complete certain tasks.

And like an older brother getting blamed when his young brother does something wrong, middle managers take the flak when the people they supervise mess up.

It can get depressing.

That's why I'm so glad Jesus understands middle management in a way few -- if any -- of us ever will.

Wanna talk about being in the middle?

Think about the position Jesus was in.

On one side was a loving God.

On the other, a sinful, fallen people.

God wanted to be reconciled with his people.

Jesus wanted to obey his father.

But he'd get crucified doing it.

Literally.

I'm sorry, but if those were my marching orders, I might have wanted to apply elsewhere.

And these were tall orders, even for the son of God.

Just listen to Christ's prayer in a garden called Gethsemane. His words can be found in the New Testament book of Mark, chapter 14.

I can almost hear the anguish in his voice as I read verse 36: "Father ... everything is possible for you. Take this cup from me...."

Sounds he like he wanted to find a different plan of action.

Then listen to what Jesus said next: "Yet not what I will, but what you will."

In other words, "I'll do what you want me to do."

Jesus could have decided to quit - surely no middle manager today would have blamed him - but he knew what he had to do the save the people he loves.

Oh well, at least Jesus could count on his inner circle for support during this tough time, right?

Now, he'd mentored a group of 12 disciples. Taught them. Ate with them. Walked with them.

So you think they'd support him, right?

Nope. They ran away.

One disciple betrayed him. Another denied even knowing him. And a third later doubted that Jesus was even alive after he rose from the dead.

Some inner circle.

OK. Perhaps Jesus could find a little compassion among those people he came to supervise, guide and help. How many people did he teach, comfort and even heal?

Surely, they'd stick up for him.

Doesn't sound like it.

I wonder how many of them were in the crowd that called out for his crucifixion. Or how many stayed quiet rather than risk trouble for themselves? Or how many figured there was nothing they could do?

There must have been times when Jesus felt so alone.

Kind of like a middle manager.

Maybe that's one reason why I love Jesus so much.

He can relate to us. He knows what it's like to feel frustrated, forgotten and forlorn. At one point on the cross, he even cried out: "My God, my God, why have you forsaken me."

Even the writer of the book of Hebrews tells how Christ can relate to all of us - from the lowest-paid worker to the head of the corporation - those of us who may feel insufficient, misunderstood, weak, tired, tempted to give up or tempted to lash out.

In chapter 4, verse 15, the author writes: "For we do not have a high priest who is unable to sympathize with our weaknesses, but we have one who has been tempted in every way, just as we are -- yet was without sin."

Christ paid the ultimate price for loyalty to his father and devotion to all of us.

No, he didn't get fired.

He died and then rose from the dead.

Now, because of his sacrifice, we have the best retirement plan we could ever ask for: eternal life.

And Jesus?

I think he got a promotion.

Look at what the Apostle Paul says in a letter to the Philippians. In chapter 2, verse 9 of the Bible, we read: "Therefore God exalted him to the highest place and gave him the name that is above every name, that at the name of Jesus every knee should bow, in heaven and on earth, and every tongue confess that Jesus Christ is Lord, to the glory of God the Father."

I don't think it gets much better than that.

Thank you for reading "Real Spiritual Spinach – Faith for the Journey"

I truly hope and pray that it has brought you comfort, peace and hope and given you an incredible hunger for God's word. Never stop reading, praying, hoping, trusting and believing.

"May the God of hope fill you with all joy and peace, as you trust in him, so that you may overflow with hope by the power of the Holy Spirit." Romans 15:13

To obtain more copies of this book for friends or relatives, please send: $17.99 or two books for $30.00 plus $3.95 for shpping and handling. And please allow 4 to 6 weeks for delivery. Please send check or money order to:

Tammy Real-McKeighan
P.O. Box 2075
Fremont, Nebraska 68026

A portion of the proceeds from the sale of this book will benefit the Royal Family Kids' Camps program.

Scriptures used throughout this book are from the New International Version of the Holy Bible; International Bible Society, East Brunswick, N.J.